Lessons in Resilience

Learning from
Loss, Uncertainty, Change, & Kinfolk

Dr. Sonia Alvarez-Robinson

Life Shift LLC

Published by
Life Shift, LLC
Atlanta, Georgia
www.whatcouldyoube.com

Library of Congress Cataloging-in-Publication Data
Names: Alvarez-Robinson, Sonia M., author
Title: Lessons in Resilience: Learning from Loss, Uncertainty, Change, and
Kinfolk
Description: Atlanta: Life Shift (2025)

Identifiers:
ISBN: 979-8-9997717-0-4 (paperback)
ISBN: 979-8-9997717-2-8 (hardback)
ISBN: 979-8-9997717-1-1 (ebook)
ISBN: 979-8-9997717-3-5 (audio)

BISAC: SEL024000 SEL031000 SELF-HELP / Personal Growth / General,
PSY003000 PSYCHOLOGY / Applied Psychology, FAM014000 FAMILY & RE-
LATIONSHIPS / Death, Grief, Bereavement

Subjects: Self-Help, Resilience, Transitions, Personal Strategy, Recovery,
Change Management, Loss, Grief, Healing, Post Traumatic Growth, Life
Planning

First Edition

Book Cover & Interior Design by Kedi Darby

To my mother, Bonita, who taught me

that I am not defined by what happens to me,

but by how I grow through what I go through.

Contents

PART 2

Fifteen Lessons for Building Resilience . . 67

Foreword

It is both an honor and a personal privilege to write the foreword for Dr. Sonia M. Alvarez-Robinson. I believe she is a living example of what it means to survive, adapt, and ultimately thrive through life's most profound challenges.

Dr. Alvarez-Robinson does not write about resilience from a distance. She writes from within loss, uncertainty, disruption, and the complex influence of kinfolk. She invites readers into deep personal experiences—not for sympathy, but to demonstrate what is possible when courage, reflection, and intention meet adversity.

What makes this book exceptional is its integration of lived experience and evidence-based insight. As a seasoned strategist and change leader, Dr. Alvarez-Robinson weaves decades of expertise in organizational development, leadership, and human systems into her personal story. She bridges research and reality, offering the Resilience FIRST Model™ not as abstract theory, but as a framework refined through both scholarship and suffering.

This book arrives at a critical time. We are living in an era marked by collective trauma, global uncertainty, social division, and rapid change. Individuals, families, organizations, and communities are navigating acute shocks and chronic stressors at unprecedented levels. In this context, resilience is not optional; it is essential.

As her mentee, I have witnessed the integrity behind these words. I have observed her lead with clarity during disruption and transform personal tragedy into professional purpose. I have seen how she empowers others to define their values, strengthen their voice, and build resilience long before crisis demands it. The wisdom offered here is not theoretical—it is embodied.

This book is more than a memoir. It is a guide and a companion for navigating life's inevitable shifts. You will recognize yourself in these chapters—in the desires that propel you forward, the discontentment that forces difficult decisions, and the disruptions that alter your path. And, if you are willing, you will also discover practical tools to use.

As you turn these pages, read with intention. Reflect honestly. Engage the exercises fully. Resilience is not built in theory; it is built in practice.

Dr. Alvarez-Robinson reminds us that while we are not defined by what happens to us, we are undeniably shaped by it. When we lean in with courage and clarity, we can emerge not only surviving—but wiser, stronger, and more aligned with our purpose.

May this book strengthen your readiness, clarify your response, and restore your spirit to equip you to bend, yet not break.

With deep respect and gratitude,
Dr. Joi Alexander

Introduction

As I reflect on the fifty-seven years I have walked this Earth, I know I am blessed to have learned many powerful lessons. The most useful and memorable came through the experiences that caused major shifts in my sense of self and the world around me. Acute shocks and chronically stressful situations such as bullying, rape, teen/single parenthood, housing instability, domestic violence, job loss, family illness (physical and mental), widowhood, spinal injury, and family estrangement have taught me so much. Through these **life shifts**, I have learned to adapt, adjust, address, and accept the reality of what is (even if it is not what I planned or wanted it to be).

I consider these experiences all part of my L.U.C.K. in life— good and bad. Through each major shift, I learned how to manage my losses, deal with uncertainty, cope with change, and understand how kinfolk shaped my worldview. In this book, I will share the strength and insight I have gained through these lessons in resilience.

Loss has taught me to appreciate life, remain engaged in the present, and simultaneously prepare for the future. Scott A. Robinson was my best friend, soulmate, and husband of thirteen years. He died at forty-seven years young, leaving behind his eighty-year-old mother Pat, our ten-year-old son Sage, and me. I felt like one of my limbs had been amputated. I limped along, struggling to find my balance. The phantom pains were excruciating. Over time, I began to heal, gaining a deeper appreciation for the temporal nature of our existence on this Earth.

After five years of widowhood, I met my second husband, Wesley, who has been an amazing addition to my life. The loss of Scott is still present, but I have learned to build a life around my grief and move forward while still honoring the past.

I am also learning to manage the fear of a loss. When I become consumed by fears and dark imaginings about anticipatory loss, I gently redirect my thoughts back to the present. Fearing loss is a natural reaction to our perception of a threat. There is real danger in the world. We must be aware of those dangers and prepare to minimize harm to ourselves and our loved ones. For years, I suffered intense anxiety, worrying about something bad happening to people I care for. It robbed me of my sleep, distracted me at work, and consumed my energy around the clock. I began to realize that projecting a future loss was stealing from the gift of my present.

Loss has taught me to live in the **now** while also being planful about the future. I don't know what tomorrow or next week will bring, but I know that I will waste the present if I am consumed by fears about the future.

Uncertainty has shown me that I can trust myself and my ability to be adaptable and optimistic. I am learning to put my energy toward what I can control when things are uncertain. When I was a twenty-one-year-old single mother of two toddler boys, I struggled to pay rent, college tuition, children's day care, food, transportation, and utility bills. I came up short most of the time. But I refused to accept being stuck in this struggle. The future was uncertain, but there was one thing I was certain about: I needed to take control of my situation and make a change. I enrolled at the community college, fell in love with learning, and went on to earn four college degrees while working my way up to a successful leadership career. Through uncertainty, I learned how to define my own life's vision rather than wait for anyone to define it for me.

Humans thrive best in environments that are safe, predictable, trustworthy, and understandable. But life often takes us down paths that do not offer those conditions. It is like driving on a steep mountain road at midnight with no streetlights. By working to build my resilience, I am putting on the high beams to illuminate the winding and unclear path ahead, while accepting that all I know for sure is this moment right now.

In Transitions, originally authored in 1980, William Bridges describes change in three stages: ending, neutral zone, and new beginnings. He artfully writes that in the neutral zone, we can get lost between the old/familiar and the new. He urges a nurturing of curiosity to ignite our ability to see new possibilities (Bridges & Bridges, 2019).

Change has opened my eyes to the possibility that I can do and be more than I have ever imagined. I heard a saying many years ago that change is inevitable, but growth is optional. I have learned that no matter how painful a change might be, new opportunities will emerge in the aftermath. Change has taught me to value the present and stay open to what might be in store for me in the future. It taught me patience and strengthened my faith that there is a plan for me that I have no control over.

In the middle of my career, I found myself out of a job due to a "strategic restructuring." Ironically, I had recommended the reorganization but never imagined that I would be impacted by it. The change was jolting and led me to question my worth. I was afraid, angry, hurt, and confused. Over time, it was revealed that the change was part of a greater plan for my life that I could not see. In retrospect, I needed that experience to get out of my comfort zone, which was necessary for growing personally and professionally. It taught me empathy and patience, and it strengthened my faith in a power greater than myself.

Kinfolk are the people in my life who have had the greatest influence on how I have been programmed. They have been my rock of support through difficult and joyous times, and a great source of strength and energy. They have also been extremely exhausting, frustrating, and disappointing.

I started this life abandoned by my birth father, condemned for my mixed-race identity, and othered by narrow-minded family and community members for much of my childhood. My mom, a brave survivor of childhood trauma, showed me what it meant to be resilient. She taught me that others' hurtful acts do not define us. I am learning not to carry the resentments, bitterness, or burdens of my kinfolk as if they were my own. I cannot change how my kinfolk have programmed me, but I can reprogram my thoughts, beliefs, and actions that do not serve me well.

> RESILIENCE
> *the ability of an individual, organization, community, or ecosystem to survive, adapt, and thrive through acute shocks and chronic stressors.*

I use the acronym L.U.C.K. as a nod to both the good and bad luck that have impacted my life. I have learned a great deal from loss, uncertainty, change, and kinfolk. I learn every time I initiate a change that leads to uncertainty and creates a challenge. I can focus on the controllables, tap into my strengths, and quiet the self-critical voice in my head begging for my attention.

My Views on Resilience

Beyond what I have gone through in my personal life, I am a professional strategist, problem solver, and change leader with more than thirty years of experience helping people navigate adversity, conflict, and change in the workplace. My two master's degrees and PhD programs focused on understanding organizational change, human development, and the influence of culture. I performed leadership roles in government, manufacturing, health care, and higher education environments, and I've worked as a consultant and trusted advisor to leaders in technology, finance, consumer products, hospitals, and higher education organizations around the globe. Over the past six years, I have been teaching a resilience-building course to college students. Through engaging these brilliant young minds, I am gaining new perspectives on leading, facilitating, teaching, and supporting individual and organizational resilience.

This book, *Lessons in Resilience*, is a collection of stories about tragedy and triumph, heartbreak and healing, breakdown and breakthrough. It offers strategies that have helped me build resilience. The definition of *resilience* that I use most is: "the ability of an individual, organization, community, or ecosystem to survive, adapt, and thrive through acute shocks and chronic stressors." I am sharing some of my most intimate stories with the desire to offer inspiration, hope, and optimism to those who may be going through difficult challenges.

The hardest times have taught me how to **access my personal power** by reaching inside myself to draw out my strengths. Through these struggles, I have come to realize that I am stronger than I ever thought I could be. People are an important part of your support system, but you also must enlist your own agency to get through difficulty. It would have been more difficult to go from poverty to prosperity without the support of my mom, friends, husbands, and colleagues. Yet my own hard work, tenacity, and grit got me through and continue to serve me well today.

I have learned that I must **bend so I don't break**. Agility, flexibility, and adaptability allow you to move when you need to. I stretch my resilience muscles by practicing resilient living in moments of calm. This helps me be limber enough to shift quickly. I can move with less pain and suffering when I am mentally, emotionally, and physically flexible. When I lost my job, I learned the importance of appreciating what you have and being ready to pivot if something is taken away.

I believe that **resilience is a state, not a trait**. You build resilience over time and through evolving experiences. It is not fixed. When I was a new widow, just getting out of bed was the furthest my resilience would take me on many days. Survival was my focus, and taking one moment, step, and day at a time was the most I could do. Resilience is a fluid and dynamic process—and the outcome of how you choose to navigate adversity and change.

Life has taught me that we can **grow through what we go through**, but it is not automatic. Traumatic events and chronic stressors do inflict pain and cause discomfort. The art of resilience is learning how to grow, not only despite these challenges, but also because of them. You are not defined by what happens to you, but you must recognize that you are always shaped by it.

Surviving rape as a teenager has always been a difficult thing for me to talk about. For years, I carried an intense shame and fear of judgment. Over time, I shared parts of the story with my closest confidants. Today, I can talk about it with young women in hopes that it will help them find self-compassion and personal strength.

The Resilience FIRST Model™ provided in Part Two of this book offers evidence-based strategies to achieve a state of resilience through life's ups and downs. Your experiences, whether the result of your own choices or circumstances outside your control, can teach you valuable lessons. The model is based on things I learned as I dug into peer-reviewed research and compared the results with my own lived experiences. It offers five strategies:

☞ Find Your Locus of Control

☞ Investigate and Manage Your Fears

☞ Reprogram Unhealthy Conditioning

☞ Seek Healthy Support

☞ Take Time for Self-Care

For each of the strategies, I share three lessons that have helped me navigate the challenges. In total, these fifteen lessons have taught me to **survive, adapt, and thrive** through acute shocks and chronic stressors. Life experiences have left me feeling both powerful and powerless, calm and overwhelmed, brave and petrified, confident and vulnerable. These experiences inspired me to develop skills, techniques, and behaviors to manage my good and bad luck.

Finding purpose as an advocate, teacher, and writer on resilience emerged as I developed healthy ways to manage my own adversity, challenges, and change. Helping others grow, learn, and find joy through life's ups and downs also strengthens my resilience.

As I write this, many things test my resilience daily. My heart aches because millions of people do not have resources to meet their basic human needs: clean water, food, sanitation, safe shelter, and health care. I am pained by our society's rigid ideological divisions, blatant hateful rhetoric, and increasing violence. I am seeing our democracy crumble as innocent people are being persecuted and killed for their identity and standing up for others. I am fearful of existential threats that seem more ominous each passing day.

Resilience is more important now than ever. I pray that this book will offer help and hope if you are struggling with experiences of loss, uncertainty, change, and kinfolk.

PART 1

Life Shifts

1

Drivers of Life's Shifts

As you reflect on the ups and downs of your life's journey, what do you notice about **why** those shifts happened? Do you find that the causes and influences of those changes vary from story to story? For me, shifts have been a combination of the choices I have made and things that have been completely out of my control. Through experiences, studies, and others' stories, I've found there are three primary drivers of shift: **desires**, **discontentment**, and **disruption**.

Your **desires** for growth, development, advancement, and success can compel you to seek a shift from where you are to where you want to be. When life is in a state of **discontentment**, you might feel like you're stuck or your pace is either too fast or too slow. If joy is missing and you aren't feeling as fulfilled as you know you deserve to be, you can feel the need to make a shift. When you experience a **disruption** in life, the shift might be out of your control and result in a shock or stressor. Let's explore these three drivers of shift in a bit more detail.

Desires

Your dreams can inspire you to make a shift from where you are to where you want to be. It is natural to desire progression. It is the essence of human development. Some shifts you initiate and control, even when you do not have complete control over the outcome.

My first professional job was working for the federal government as a clerk typist, processing the paperwork of federally insured homes that had gone into foreclosure. I was making $5.50 an hour, scraping together money every month to pay for rent, food, gas, clothes, day care, and other essentials. I longed for a career in which I would make enough to take care of my children without stress. I applied for higher-paying roles but was denied advancement because I did not have a college education or experience in any other roles. I knew I had to gain new experiences and get an education.

I enrolled at Minneapolis Community and Technical College, taking night and weekend classes. I will never forget the first advisement meeting. The advisor was adamant that I take a core set of classes before I could delve into things that were in my area of interest.

"English Composition 101. That is where you need to start," he said.

I was disappointed because I wanted to take classes on social justice and human relations in the workplace.

"There will be time for that," he replied. "But first, you need to know how to write like a college student."

I took the English class, and about three-quarters of the way through the course, the instructor asked me, "Where did you learn to write like this?"

I explained that for most of my teenage years, I was grounded from seeing friends or watching TV as punishment for my rebellious behavior. Writing was my outlet. That was the first time I recognized how solitary confinement was a benefit to my life.

"I bet if you submit these papers you wrote for this class to a local publication, they will print them," my professor urged.

I scoffed at this suggestion, but I gave it a try anyway. Little did I realize that this action, inspired by my first college professor, would forever change the trajectory of my professional life. Of the five papers I submitted, three were published. Even more rewarding than the publicity was the $50 I was paid for each paper! I used that money toward my tuition the following semester and began to build my brand as someone interested in culture, inclusion, and human dynamics.

One of the articles, "Defining Culture, It's More Than Skin Deep," published by La Prensa de Minnesota in 1994, caught the attention of Steven Zachary, the director of the Office of Diversity and Equal Opportunity for the State of Minnesota, who called me at work.

"I read your article on identity and culture, and I like how you think," he said. "I lead the state office of diversity, and we are looking for someone to join our team. Would you be interested in applying for this role?"

He explained that the role was funded for only one year, with the potential to be renewed each year. As a single mother with two little boys to care for, I was reluctant to leave my stable federal government job, even though it was low pay with limited advancement. Steven was offering a salary $10,000 more than I was making. I needed to explore my options.

I placed a call to Marvin, a high-ranking leader of the agency I worked for. I'd met him through a training program earlier that year and he told me that if I ever needed advice, I could call on him. I described the opportunity before me, along with the risks of taking a temporary role.

"Do you know that the federal government has a provision that allows employees to take up to two years leave of absence to pursue new knowledge or experience?" he shared. "You could request the leave of absence and take the job. You can come back within the next two years without losing your service credits or having to start over. You will just need approval from your local office leadership."

I had no idea that was even possible! I thanked Marvin and quickly went to work on writing my request to our local office manager. My request explained how the agency would benefit from my new experiences in conflict resolution, employee engagement, and inclusive workplaces. I would return with new skills, ready to contribute even more.

I reviewed my letter several times to make sure it met the provision's criteria. I got along well with my supervisor, so I expected her to be sympathetic to my request. Unfortunately, she was not. She shot it down like a hunter kills a duck in open season.

"We can't afford to hold your position for two years," she said. Mavis was a short, stocky woman in her early fifties who wore Lee jeans, sneakers, and plaid button-down shirts to work almost every day.

"The policy says you don't have to hold my position but that I must be able to come back in the same grade in any position. Surely there will be entry-level clerk positions open in the future," I pleaded.

"The answer is no." She pursed her lips. "And that's final."

I sat with slumped shoulders, hanging my head in disappointment. How could they deny me this opportunity after five years of dedicated service? I decided to appeal this decision and wrote a letter to Mavis's boss, Sally. Surely, I thought, she would see the reasonableness of my logic and approve the request. I sheepishly approached her office, afraid of being rejected again.

"Come in," she said. I sat in the metal frame chair with 1970s-style pea-green cushions. "While I admire what you are trying to do, we just can't allow it." She smiled. "What kind of agency would we have if we let everyone just take two years off? It's just not possible."

While that was not the answer I was looking for, it was the answer I needed. At that moment, I decided to leave anyway—and never wanted to return. They did not value me as a person, only as a set of tasks to be performed. I called Marvin back to let him know I would be resigning and thank him for being a great advisor.

"Hold on," he said, "Don't resign yet. Let me make a few calls. Just sit tight."

Within about an hour, I heard a door slam. It came from Sally's office. Then she emerged from around a corner, face beet-red, fists clenched, and a deep scowl on her brow. At first, it appeared she was heading toward me. But then she took a sharp military turn left and went out the door.

Everyone in the cube farm stared at the door in disbelief. What just happened?

Then my phone rang. It was Marvin. "Congratulations," he said. "You just got approval to take a two-year developmental leave of absence."

I could hardly contain my excitement, but I could feel the sharp beams of disdain piercing me from across the room. Mavis wasn't happy about it either.

I did not gloat. In fact, I reserved my celebration for when I got home that day.

When it comes to shifts inspired by your desires, you may have complete control over initiating the shift, but you might not control the experience or the outcome. Pursuing new learning and growth represents a shift that creates not only new opportunities but also new challenges. I learned that I must prepare for everything that comes with a shift inspired by my desires.

Discontentment

Many people wander through life, only to find themselves looking back in their later years and wondering where the time went. In his doctoral research on aging, one of my most influential mentors, Randall, surveyed octogenarians (people over eighty) by asking them a simple question: "If you could change one thing about how you lived your life, what would it be?"

Participants in the study had two common responses. First, many said they would not have settled for situations and relationships that were unsatisfying; they would have **taken more risks**.

Secondly, they said they would have been **more intentional** in how they lived. Resoundingly, they echoed the sentiment that life is too short to be in any relationship, job, environment, community, or situation that is not fulfilling.

Early in my adulthood, before I met my loving husband Scott, I was in a relationship with a man who was physically, emotionally, and verbally abusive to me. I hesitated to leave him because I always blamed myself for what was happening to me. I did not know my own worth. He said he was sorry and did nice things for me after being mean and physically violent. I often kept a kitchen knife nearby to defend myself if I needed it. I was drawn to the drama, and I didn't think I could do any better. I tried to say and do all the "right" things to avoid provocation. I wore what he wanted me to wear, isolated myself from my friends, and was always available when he needed me. I didn't dare complain when he stayed out with other women overnight. I went to work every day, never letting my co-workers know what I was going through.

I was discontented, but not enough to change—until it reached the breaking point. One late afternoon, I was folding clothes as my one- and three-year-old boys played nearby. He came home and was hungry. He demanded I get downstairs and fix something for him to eat. I wasn't moving fast enough, so he shoved me between my shoulder blades. I plummeted down the stairs, blacking out on the way down.

I woke up dazed with my three-year-old sitting on my chest, shaking me and calling, "Mommy, Mommy! Are you dead?"

After that, I knew I needed to shift. I was finally discontented enough to act. I only wished I had done it much sooner.

When you initiate a change, like getting out of a bad situation, it can be stressful and frightening. Fear of the unknown, adjustment of learning, and doing something new can cause anxiety. Letting go of things that are familiar, even if they are unfulfilling or harmful, can be difficult. Many of us believe the saying "The devil we know is better than the one we don't know." This falsehood lies deep in the subconscious and causes people to stay stagnant in unhealthy, unrewarding, and unfulfilling situations, even when they don't realize it.

If you are feeling discontented, this book will help you confront the fears that may be holding you hostage and create a plan for navigating unfamiliar terrain.

Being resilient does not mean tolerating unhealthy situations or environments because you can tough it out. Sometimes, it means loving yourself enough to move on when the situation is not in your best interests.

Disruption

Globally, nationally, organizationally, and individually, disruption is active and relentless. The word disruption is often used to describe innovation and change, such as Uber's disruption of the taxi industry and Amazon's disruption of the brick-and-mortar retail industry. In an age of rapid technological advancement, the pace of change is accelerating at a rate that exceeds human capacity to adapt to that change. Although this kind of disruption invariably leads to progress, there are consequences to human experiences.

Disruption occurs in every part of life. A new circumstance can be thrust upon you whether you like it or not—and whether you are ready or not. In a split second, everything you have been counting on can be disrupted. A health diagnosis, a natural disaster, the breakup of a serious relationship, a new baby, the death of a loved one—there are so many things that can disrupt your way of life and force you to shift.

When I was thirty-two years old, I achieved my goal to marry an amazing life partner who was the perfect husband. Yes, it was a goal I had written down! Scott Robinson was handsome, brilliant, kind, honest, and so committed to his family. He loved me and fully accepted my boys, David and Alonzo, who were seven and nine years old when we met. We dated for three years before we married in 2000. Two years later, we were blessed with a third son, Sage.

Things were so good that I would often pinch myself to make sure my life wasn't a dream. My friends secretly thought I was exaggerating our joy. But it was real—a fairy tale romance envied by many.

In our thirteenth year of wedded bliss, Scott went in for hip replacement surgery. It was three days before Mother's Day. On the day of the surgery, I told him how nervous I was.

"God makes no mistakes, Sonia," he reassured me. "Once I get this hip fixed, we can dance all night. I want to take my son camping. I want to walk the golf course without hurting. I just want to live a better life."

I tried to be optimistic, but I knew the risks he was taking in having this surgery. Scott was born with a genetic blood disorder called sickle cell disease, which caused life-threatening health events when his body experienced stress of any kind. Certainly, hip replacement surgery fell into that category. Just two years prior, he'd had the same surgery on the other hip, and it caused a major sickle cell crisis. He barely survived that episode after being in the ICU for two weeks.

The second surgery seemed to go well, and he went immediately into recovery. He was up and walking around with the help of a physical therapist the very next day. On the third day, I left him in the care of the nurses and took our youngest son to the school carnival. By midday, I got a call from Scott, asking me to return to the hospital. The unusually feeble tone of his voice told me he was in danger.

When I got there, I found his hospital room door closed and he was screaming in pain. I went to look for a nurse and found a heavyset woman named Rita, who was responsible for his care.

"He's just being a big baby," she had the nerve to tell me.

"He is having a sickle cell crisis!" I replied with an elevated pitch in my voice.

I argued with her to get him the dosage level of morphine he needed for pain relief. She refused. I was getting nowhere with her, so I started calling the doctor's offices. It was Saturday, and I desperately pleaded with their answering services to get the doctors to call me right away.

Finally, after six hours of begging for someone to get him the care he needed, they moved him up to the ICU to get the dosage of pain management required for a sickle cell crisis. Unfortunately, this needless suffering is common among sickle cell patients who face health care practices rooted in biased perceptions that they are seeking drugs to get high. Most sickle cell patients are of African descent and face prejudice—even from people who look like them.

By the time Scott was moved out of the orthopedic ward and into the ICU, his blood pressure was sky high, and his heart was racing. This was the beginning of his six-week fight for his life. During a sickle cell crisis, the red blood cells get sticky and clump up. They can't carry precious oxygen to the major organs. His kidneys and liver were both failing. His heart showed signs of distress. The intensive care unit was full of patients, and the ICU nurses were managing two patients each, many of them just as sick as Scott.

After a week of his status being touch and go, something woke me from a dead sleep at 3:00 a.m. I was lying across the countertop in Scott's room, where my friend Vonetta had created a makeshift bed for me. The telemetry alarm was going off. The red lights were blinking, but the alarms were silent. The nurses had muted the volume so the sound wouldn't annoy them. As I cleared my eyes, I saw the blurry screen of the monitor that registered heart rate, blood pressure, and oxygen levels.

All were at zero!

I jumped to his bedside and felt his stiff body. His heart had stopped, and he wasn't breathing. I ran out of the room to find help but there was no one in sight. The nursing station with monitoring screens was unattended. After several minutes I finally found a nurse whom I had never seen before. I led her to the room where she pushed the code blue button. Then she started CPR and a team of hospital workers in blue scrubs arrived within a few minutes.

I crumpled to the floor, sobbing uncontrollably. After several minutes, a nurse came over and put her hand on my shoulder. "We brought him back," she said with a half-smile. I could tell that it was still not good news. Later, I learned that too much time had lapsed between his heart stopping and restarting. His brain had been deprived of oxygen and damaged beyond repair.

I was relieved that they had revived him, even though he was barely hanging on and depended on a ventilator for every single breath.

For three more weeks, I massaged his lifeless limbs and whispered words of encouragement into his ears. Our close friends Charlotte and Kymm traveled from Maryland to check on us. Reverend Frazier flew from Minnesota to pray over him. Scott's friends Henry and Jerry came to encourage him to hold on. But he just lay there, eyes wide open, unable to speak. He was also unable to make deliberate movements or interact on any level.

As Scott lay there, clinging to life, I was afraid to leave his side. I didn't trust the nurses or doctors to do what was in his best interests. My friends Sandi and Murielle—a doctor and a nurse—both confirmed my fears about the lack of quality care. We all took turns making sure he was cared for properly.

The trauma continued until June 14, 2013, when his breathing became rapid, and his gaze fixed on me.

"You can go, baby," I whispered to him. "I will see you on the other side."

After forty-five minutes of gasping breaths, a nurse finally arrived. "I will get the cart!" she exclaimed.

I shook my head slowly. "No, let him go," I replied.

Scott was dead at forty-seven years old, two days before Father's Day. Our youngest son, Sage, was only ten. I stood in the room with his lifeless body, struggling to imagine how I would tell my children that Scott was not coming home again. I tried to imagine what counsel Scott would give me. I imagined him saying, "How would you advise your clients in this moment?" I reflected on my work helping people deal with unpleasant, unplanned changes and the advice I gave to many leaders.

Talking aloud to myself, I said, "Sonia, you need to first build their confidence in you as their leader. They need to know that you have the skills, the knowledge, and the strength to lead them through this difficult time. Secondly, you need to help them see a new future. It is hard enough to let go. They need something close and immediate that they can anchor their minds and hearts to. Thirdly, as impossible as it may be to imagine, they need to know there will be some good that comes from this very difficult experience. Something beautiful is in store for their future. And finally, you must let them grieve. Sorrow, pain, and heartache are all part of experiencing loss. Whether that loss is a job, a spouse, a child, or a home, it is hard to lose someone or something you love."

After this long conversation with myself (which must have worried the nurses), I stood in the hospital room with Scott for the last time. I knew I must own this major life shift. By the time my dear friend Sandi arrived to comfort me, my head was clear, and I was ready to lead my family through a new, difficult chapter.

The loss still leaves a hole in my heart. I miss him deeply, even twelve years later. Yet it gave me the drive to help other people navigate loss and unplanned change. My experience of widowhood also made me a more effective change management practitioner in my professional life. The empathy and compassion I have for others has increased through this experience.

You may be reading this because you are experiencing a disruptive time. You might need affirmation that it will be okay in the end. Most people are thrown off track when they experience a major unplanned change. It is important to give yourself grace and cut yourself some slack. It can take time to put things back in order when you have a disruption.

Summary

Shift is inevitable, whether to fulfill your desires, resolve discontentment, or adapt to a disruption. During these shifts, your self-confidence may get shaken, you may fear the worst, and you may have dark imaginings of the unknown. These are all completely normal and common reactions to shift.

Yet it is important to know that growth, deeper meaning, and astounding joy are possible on the other side of that change. This book will get you ready for any kind of shift so you can thrive through change and find joy through life's unpredictable journey.

Self-Reflection Activity:
THE ROLLER-COASTER RIDE

Life is a series of upshifts and downshifts. Like a winding mountain road or a theme-park thrill ride, the momentum we build by climbing higher can also be followed by a terrifying plummet.

In this exercise, you will reflect on the highs and the lows of the experiences that have mattered the most. Consider the shifts your desires, discontentment, or disruptions have caused.

Follow these three steps for this roller-coaster ride exercise:

Step 1: Brainstorm. Make a list of the experiences that have shaped your life and your perspectives the most. For each one, indicate whether it was a high point (joyous), a low point (painful), or a neutral point.

SHIFTS *What was the shift?* *What was the cause?*	**QUALITY OF** **THE EXPERIENCE** *Was it a high, low or neutral point?*

Step 2: Plot the items. After you have created your list, plot each item as a point on a chart that has two axes: horizontal/time (the chronological order of these major events) and vertical/quality (if it was a high, neutral, or low point experience). My example is shown below.

My Rollercoster Ride

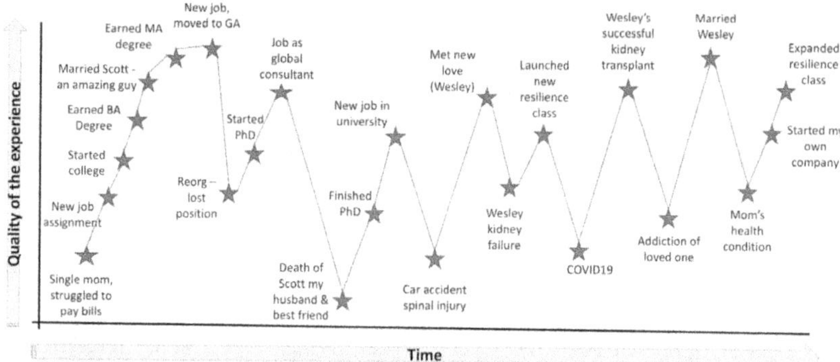

Figure 1. My Life's Roller-Coaster Ride

Step 3: Reflect. After you plot each item from your list on the chart, take a moment to reflect on these experiences.

☞ What did you learn about yourself and others through the highs and lows?

☞ What helped you bounce back from the low points?

☞ How did these experiences influence how you deal with adversity and challenges today?

☞ What positive outcomes did you experience following adversity (e.g., greater sense of personal strength, greater appreciation for life, ability to see new possibilities, more meaningful relationships, stronger spiritual connections)?

2

Three Phases of Resilience

Resilience is developed and harnessed in three phases.

Readiness for shifts prepares you for the range of highs and lows life brings. You can build your readiness for the difficulties ahead without catastrophizing about the worst-case scenario.

Response to shifts resiliently involves managing your reaction to what has happened to you or around you. Even if you do not have control over the cause of a shift, you can control your response and do it in healthy and productive ways.

Recovery from shifts is an often-overlooked part of building resilience. It is about taking time to regenerate, reset, and refuel your body, mind, and spirit. The formula for resilience is shown in the diagram below. Building resilience happens through your actions in three phases.

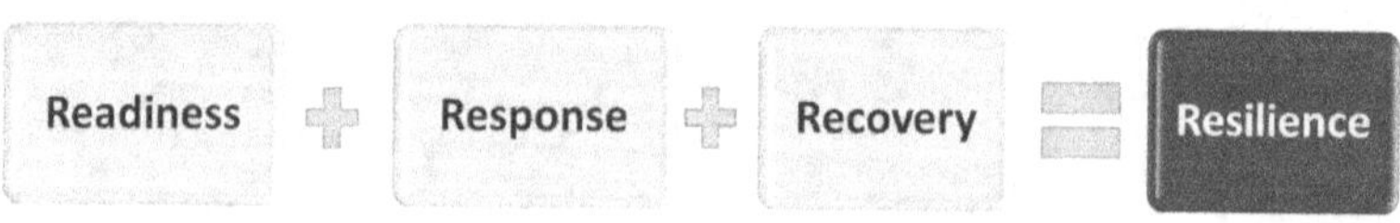

Figure 2. Three Phases to Build Resilience

Readiness

It can be challenging to prepare for adversity and change without creating unnecessary worry, fear, and anxiety. I can be a master catastrophizer, spinning a worst-case scenario story in my head faster than you can blink. As I build my resilience, I am learning to prepare for adverse situations without becoming obsessed by them.

Consider preparing for a severe weather event. You can't control the weather, but you can plan your activities around what is predicted and secure any supplies you need to get through the storm. The Disaster Preparedness Model developed by the American Red Cross is a great tool to help prepare for a range of potential threats. On their webpage titled "How to Prepare for Emergencies", they provide eight steps to prepare for a range of emergencies, including natural disasters, home fires, and other situations. This helpful resource equips people with knowledge, tools, and skills to effectively prepare for an emergency. While the Red Cross also provides disaster response and recovery services, they explain that preparation is essential for effective response and quick recovery. Readiness requires you to be willing to accept the reality of a potential change or adverse situation before it happens.

My early lessons about readiness for adversity began more than thirty years ago when I was a single mother making $5.50 an hour and paying $3 of that toward childcare. The remainder went to rent, food, utilities, and repairs to my rusty, old Plymouth Duster that sputtered and choked as it took me to and from work. We lived in a subsidized housing community where everyone was struggling financially. Many of my neighbors relied on "alternative economies" to get by.

One afternoon, as I was unloading the boys from the back seat of my rust-bucket after a long day at work, I noticed a group of adults near the playground. I did not recognize them and could not see what they were doing until I got closer. As I approached the playground area, I realized that a woman was performing a sex act on one of the men, and the others were gathered around, watching. I whisked my boys swiftly past them and into the house.

That was it! We had to get out of there.

I had to get ready to make a move and do it fast. I set a plan to increase my earnings and get into a better living situation. Sitting at our little kitchen table, I wrote out all the legit ways I could make more money without sacrificing too much time with my boys. I reflected on how I might build on what I already knew.

My main job was processing the paperwork for foreclosed homes, and I interacted quite a bit with the real estate agents who sold the homes. They taught me about the industry that supported the foreclosure experience. People were making good money preparing these homes to be sold on the market. Why couldn't I do that? I did my research to make sure it would not be a conflict of interest. If I subcontracted with authorized real estate companies that sold bank-owned foreclosures, I could do it without breaking any rules.

At twenty-three, I created my first side hustle—a small business called Alvarez Mops Up. On weekends, I took my boys and a playpen with their favorite toys to vacant homes, where I would clean while they played quietly. After about six months of doing this work, I was hired to clean a four-bedroom, two-story home in a quiet neighborhood in North Minneapolis. The moment I walked through the door, I knew it was the house for me.

I cleaned it with diligent attention and effort. Despite the vandalism throughout most of the house, I could see the potential. The rich wood crown molding and intricately carved, built-in mahogany cabinet gave it a warm charm. The spacious living and dining room area would be perfect for playing games, dancing, and having family fun. I just knew I had to have it—and I had been getting ready for this change.

The home was a bank-owned property with a remaining mortgage of $45,000. That was the amount the bank wanted to take off their hands. I would need $1,350 for the down payment and credit approval for a mortgage. My credit was marred by poor decisions I had made as a young adult. However, the bank expressed a conditional willingness to work with me if I paid off all outstanding debts. I had been able to save only $1,500, despite the number of hours I had been working. My savings were enough to pay off my past debts, but that left me nothing for the down payment. The clock was ticking on the offer, and the bank was going to hold the property for me for only another two weeks.

When I went to visit my grandma in the nursing home, she offered to help me with the funds. I knew she didn't have much money, so I was reluctant to take anything from her.

"I will pay you back just as soon as I can," I promised.

She wrote me a check for $1,350 and told me gently, "Use the money you have to pay off your past debts. If the bank approves your loan, you can cash this check for your down payment."

I was so grateful. I completed all the paperwork for the mortgage application and paid off my past debts.

I was awaiting final approval for the loan when I got a call from my mom.

"Did you cash the check?" she asked with an anxious tone.

"No, why?" I responded.

"Grandma had a heart attack and is in the hospital. They don't think she is going to make it. Go cash the check," my mother ordered.

"I don't want to cash the check. I want to go see Grandma," I replied.

After she continued urging, I cashed the check on my way to the hospital. My grandma died later that night.

The very next day, I received a call from my loan officer.

"You're approved," he said gleefully.

It was bittersweet. I missed my grandma, and I wished she was there to celebrate with me. I believe it was more than coincidental that her wish for me was granted the day after she left this Earth. I was so thankful to have had a support system to help me drive the needed change in my life.

This experience taught me that I can get ready amid adversity. I learned that to be ready, I had to focus on what I could control and take charge of changing my circumstances. I had to put in the effort to gain knowledge, skills, and sweat equity. I learned the value of healthy relationships and knowing when to ask for help. I put in the effort, and having my mom and grandma in my life made a big difference in the outcome.

Being a struggling single mom taught me many other lessons about readiness, such as having a stash of essentials for survival. I began to store drinking water just in case our water got shut off for nonpayment. I stocked up on rice, pasta, and canned items so I could create a "struggle meal" when we started running out of food. I planned routes to conserve gas and kept an empty gas can in the trunk because my gauge was usually close to E.

Although my financial situation has changed since then, I still stock up on food and drinking water in case our central supply becomes compromised, contaminated, or unavailable. I don't stress or obsess about the potential risk of not having access to clean and safe water. I just prepare for the potential that we won't.

Self-Reflection Activity:
READINESS FOR SHIFT

For this exercise, you will prepare for changes, challenges, or adversities that you are likely to experience. Follow these steps to complete this activity:

Step 1: Create a list of shifts that you anticipate might be in your future.

Step 2: Consider the driver of each shift. What is the cause of the shift? Is it something within your control?

Step 3: Then, identify the ways you can get ready to effectively manage that shift.

An example is provided below for your reference.

EXPECTED SHIFT	SHIFT DRIVER	HOW CAN I GET READY?
Example: Increased health risks associated with getting older	Chronology and biology	– Embrace getting older as a gift (it beats the alternative). – Get regular preventive health screenings. – Eat healthier and exercise more.
EXPECTED SHIFT	SHIFT DRIVER	HOW CAN I GET READY?

Response

When most people think of resilience, they often focus on how we respond to adverse circumstances. That is because resilience shows up nakedly in how we deal with challenges as they emerge.

Even shifts you initiate (a new job, moving to a new place, a new relationship) can evoke anxiety, stress, and fear. How you respond to shifts can significantly determine their impact and result. If you overreact, you can make a bad situation worse. If you avoid dealing with something that requires your attention, it can become a festering problem that is more difficult to deal with.

It is like driving on a slippery roadway. The last thing you want to do is slam the brakes or change directions too quickly. You will spin out, lose control, and end up in the ditch or worse. If you notice that your car is making an unusual sound and ignore it, you could be stranded on the roadside. If you have a fender bender, you can't freak out or go into a rage. Response is about accepting and addressing your realities in healthy ways that will keep you moving in a positive direction.

I learned a valuable lesson through a shift I experienced when I was forty years old. I had achieved my goal to have a successful career facilitating organizational improvement. I had earned a bachelor's degree in human resources and a master's degree in human development while working full-time and raising my boys. After more than a decade of hard work and determination, I'd established a fulfilling career as the head of strategy development and implementation for a public health agency. My responsibilities for the organization were significant, as I reported to the head of the department and led a team of fifty highly talented professionals.

I had recently led their strategic planning effort, redefining the model and structure for a new organizational future. I recommended that roles and positions be better aligned to achieve their new vision and goals. One day, I was home taking care of a sick child when I received a call from my boss.

"We have taken your advice and are going to reorganize. We have changed your role and decided it would be better performed by someone else. You still have a job, but we're not sure what we want to do with you. For now, you will not have a title or any leadership responsibilities. All your team members will report to the new person." He sounded as if he were reading a script.

Stunned, I flopped down into a chair, nearly dropping the phone. This was the first time my career didn't go according to my plan. I had goals! I'd written them down! How could the company just take that away from me? I had invested so much in my career. It was the center of my identity (outside of being a mom). Not having a title challenged me to question my identity and purpose.

Thankfully, five years prior, I had participated in a powerful leadership development program led by a petite and spunky psychologist named Violet Arnold. Her program was called Double Dutch. The program name was coined from a rope jumping game where the players must hop over two ropes swinging overhead in opposite directions. This was her metaphor for the reality that many people of diverse backgrounds face. We must navigate the overlapping identities of who we **are** and what we **do**. Her philosophy that "the **work** ethic and the **worth** ethic are inseparable" taught us to become self-directed, self-managed, and self-empowered.

The Double Dutch foundational development experience gave me the perspective and tools to take control of my reaction to any difficult situation. Violet gave us many frameworks to apply in our personal and professional lives. One stood out as most crucial at that time. She taught us that there are three dimensions of our existence: "I Do," "I Have," and "I Am."

Figure 3. Dimensions of Our Existence

I had been so focused on the "I Do" (my responsibilities, accomplishments, and activities) and the "I Have" (my possessions, status, relationships), that when I had to introduce myself (my "I Am") without those things, I was at a loss for words.

I went into deep meditation and centered my energy on trying to clarify my "I Am." Who **am I** if it is not my job title and responsibilities? The more I meditated, prayed, and listened, the clearer my "**I Am**" became.

The message from my Higher Power came back to me so clearly: "You are a resilient woman who has a passion for helping others. You can use this experience to help other people manage unplanned change and be their best under difficult circumstances."

I had to have this experience to understand the impact of unplanned change so I could empathize effectively. At the urging of my mentor Randall, I decided to pursue my PhD with a focus on leadership, culture, and organizational change. I enrolled in the doctorate in human and organizational systems program at Fielding Graduate University and began to study in earnest. The loss led to more success than I would have had without it.

I accepted that losing my position was part of my life's plan. I showed up to an empty office every day, even though I had no duties. I studied, learned, planned, and prepared for what was in store for me next. I leaned heavily on my mentor Randall to keep me from overreacting and to find constructive things for me to do. I called on Violet to provide additional mentorship throughout the process. At the same time, I explored other employment options.

About eight months after I was ousted from my role, the highest-ranking person in the organization summoned me to her office.

"We like how you handled the reorganization. You didn't turn negative, and you kept your head down and showed up every day. We weren't sure how we wanted to use your talent, but we have now figured it out. I would like for you to be my director of communications and public relations," she said matter-of-factly.

"Thank you so much for the honor," I replied. "It sounds like a great opportunity. However, just this morning, I accepted a position with a global consulting company. I'll be helping them manage change."

I tried not to gloat, but it did feel vindicating. I was blessed to have guidance from mentors, grace from God, diligence in clarifying my purpose, and resilience to pivot to fulfill my purpose in new ways. As a result, that painful experience transformed into one of the best things that ever happened to me.

From this experience, I learned that title, authority, and position are surface indicators of value. Value should be measured by our thoughts, words, and actions that benefit ourselves and others. I also learned how much self-esteem is challenged when change happens **to** us.

I also realized how important it is to have a spiritual channel to process these experiences. My relationship with my Higher Power was significantly strengthened by my forced introspection into the purpose and value of my life.

Many times, while I was in this state of flux, I questioned my own worth and competence. But over time, with support from mentors, loved ones, and my Higher Power, I developed the ability to focus my energy and attention on those things that are within my control. It became clear to me that I could not control other people's ideas, actions, decisions, or words. I could control only my response to the things that impacted me.

Owning our shift allows us to focus our response on the things that we have control over. Finding healthy and productive ways to respond to shifts (especially those that happen to us) requires intentionality. The continuum diagram below describes a range of instinctive go-to responses people often gravitate toward when living through a shift.

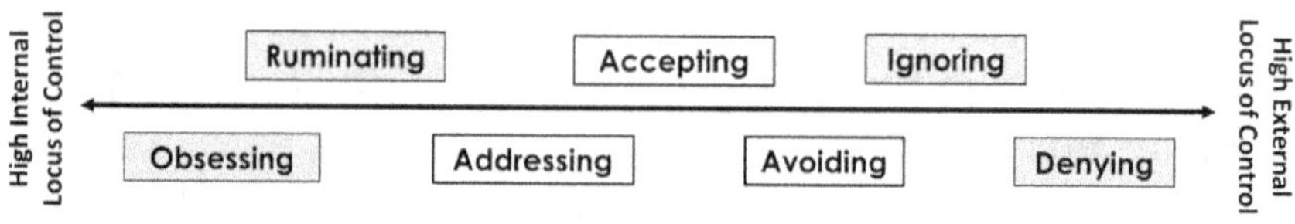

Figure 4. Range of Responses to Shift

1. **Obsessing**: Getting completely fixated on solving the problem and being unable to let go of the parts of the situation that are outside your control.

2. **Ruminating**: Replaying in your mind the bad things that could happen in the future or the negative things that have happened in the past.

3. **Addressing**: Taking measured steps to understand and begin to resolve the parts of the situation that are in your control, releasing those things that are outside your control, and seeking support as needed.

4. **Accepting**: Recognizing the shift, seeing how it impacted you, and preparing to take healthy and intentional actions, even if you don't like the situation.

5. **Avoiding**: Choosing to not deal with the situation right away so you can gather information, ideas, or perspective needed for an effective response.

6. **Ignoring**: Trying to block the situation out of your mind or choosing not to deal with it at all.

7. **Denying**: Creating an alternative reality in your mind, convincing yourself that the adversity is not real or that it is completely different than what it is.

This scale is an adaptation from the seminal work of pioneering psychologist Julian Rotter, who developed our modern understanding of the concept of locus of control (Rotter, 1954). A person with a high <u>internal</u> locus of control carries a belief that outcomes in life are the result of one's own actions, decisions, and efforts. If you have a high <u>external</u> locus of control, you believe that outcomes are largely determined by external forces, like fate, luck, or other people. These are belief sets that are programmed in our minds over time through our kinfolk, social experiences, observations, and media.

If your lived experience shows that you have the power to control the outcomes of your life, and those experiences are validated by messaging from caregivers, educators, peers, and others, you are likely to develop a high internal locus of control. However, if your life shows that you are powerless over your circumstances, and you are told the same, you are inclined to adopt a high external locus of control.

Martin Seligman coined the term "learned helplessness" to describe how persistent failure or uncontrollable stressors result in feelings of powerlessness, decreased problem-solving, emotional distress, and reduced resilience (Seligman, 1967).

Understanding your beliefs about your locus of control can illuminate your instinctive go-to responses to adversity. When you see where you tend to lean on the continuum of responses, you can manage the impact of your reactions and find healthy ways to cope.

If you have a high internal locus of control, you can leverage it as a strength by taking ownership of a situation while being aware of obsessing or ruminating in unhealthy ways. Conversely, if you have been conditioned toward a higher external locus of control, you should be aware when you ignore or deny challenges that you have the power to address. This behavior can lead to problems getting bigger and harder to solve down the line.

The healthiest and most productive ways to respond to adversity are accepting, addressing, and sometimes avoiding (when you need a moment to get a grip).

Social psychologist Albert Bandura described self-efficacy as "People's beliefs in their efficacy to manage their own functioning and to exercise control over events that affect their lives" (Bandura, 1997, p. 2). This is an essential element of addressing adverse situations in healthy and productive ways. When you believe in your own personal power, you can manage intrusive thoughts and reduce distress as they arise. Self-efficacy is foundational to human agency and influences cognition, motivation, emotion, and decision-making. High self-efficacy promotes resilience and adaptive functioning.

Self-Reflection Activity:
RESPONDING TO SHIFT

For this exercise, you will build self-awareness about your instinctive "go-to" reactions, and how they can help or hinder your ability to cope with adverse situations. There are three steps in this activity:

Step 1: Take the free internal locus of control test on Psychology Today: https://www.psychologytoday.com/us/tests/personality/locus-of-control-test

Step 2: Look at the continuum below and reflect on how you commonly respond to adversity.

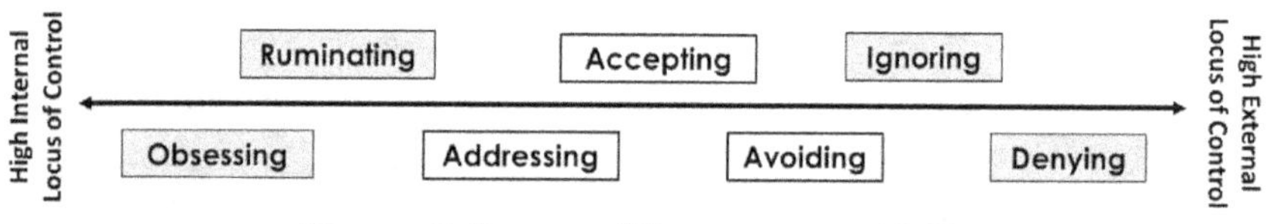

Figure 5. Range of Responses to Shift

Step 3: Consider strategies for using locus of control as a strength and mitigating conditioning that does not serve you well.

An example is provided here for your reference.

LOCUS OF CONTROL	YOUR RESPONSES	STRATEGIES
What do you notice about your locus of control beliefs? Where do they come from?	What are your common responses to acute shocks or chronic stressors?	How can your go-to be a strength while managing unhealthy responses?
Example: *The assessment shows that I have a high internal locus of control. My mom showed me to find my agency and told me that I could do anything I put my mind to.*	*I sometimes get stuck in obsessing and ruminating about problems, especially when they are out of my control. It can be all-consuming and make it challenging to function in other parts of my life.*	*I need to pay attention to when I am clinging to things that are not mine to solve. I need to focus on my responsibilities and let go of those that are not.*

Recovery

The recovery phase in building resilience is often overlooked. We often think of resilience as just grinding through hard times with grit and perseverance. While that is part of it, resilience also involves being intentional and regenerative after experiencing acute shocks and chronic stressors.

On life's road trip, you might encounter someone else's road rage, have an accident or flat tire, or run out of gas. When these things happen, you have to stop and regroup. It may require some deep breathing to calm your nerves, get a fresh tank of gas, or change a tire to get back on the road. The pause is key. It is not giving up—it is restoration.

I recently had hip replacement surgery and took six weeks off from work to recover from the shock my body experienced. Physical therapy and rehabilitation were intensive and required dedicated effort. I was fortunate that I could take that time off, and I am certain that my successful healing was due to the dedicated recovery that I was privileged to engage in. Many people cannot afford to take extended time off to heal from any injury or illness. As a result, they never fully recover. If halting the grind of your life is not possible, you might instead create periods of intentional action to restore your body, mind, and spirit from whatever insult or injury it has sustained.

In the two months following Scott's death, I defended my doctoral dissertation, held two funeral ceremonies (one in Atlanta and another in our hometown of Minneapolis), and drove to Arlington, Virginia for my doctoral graduation. I stayed busy in those first months, but I knew I had to finish what I started. I had been working on my doctoral degree for almost seven years while working as a full-time consultant and struggling to be the best wife and mother I could be. During my commencement speech, I shared my reflections about my loss, but also about what I had gained:

Five weeks ago, my champion, my soulmate, left this Earth.

He took his last breath. As I am rejoicing, I am so grate-

ful that I had thirteen wonderful years with him. While I

am sad that he is not here physically, I am such a better

person for all that he gave me. The thing that he taught me that was so powerful was to appreciate every moment. Not just every day, but every moment. Every time that the clock would turn 1:11 or 11:11, he would send me a text '1111' or '111.' It meant … you are my number one, you are the only one, we are one and we have a little one. We often joked that his major was leisure studies. While I was always focused on achievement and getting four college degrees, he was always focused on relationships. I often told him that what I do maintains us, but what he does sustains us. So, if there is one thing that I learned the most that I can leave with you is that—while it is good to have an end to journey toward, it's the journey that counts in the end.

I posted this speech to YouTube as a tribute to Scott. It was not only my academic commencement but also the commencement of my journey toward becoming a champion for resilience. This was a key part of my recovery.

After graduation, I kept pushing through even though I was exhausted and still in a fog from the shock of the loss. I went back to work as a global management consultant with clients across the country. At the time, I did not realize that grieving is part of recovery and that when our bodies, minds, and souls are injured through the loss of a loved one, we must let ourselves grieve deeply—but without getting stuck.

About three months after Scott's death, I was invited to speak at the Annual Sickle Cell Candlelight Vigil on the steps of the state capitol, where I paid honor to Scott and shared a bit about his resilience through this poem:

God Makes No Mistakes:
A Tribute to Scott A. Robinson

You were a beautiful baby,
born in a time that was not ready for you.
Through childhood, you withstood painful episodes,
the cause of your anguish invisible to others.
Doctors said you might not make it past two,
but you knew better.
And God made no mistake.
They told you not to play contact sports
so you insisted on trying out for football.
Again, they predicted a lifespan less than 10
until you celebrated your eighteenth birthday.
Graduate from college? They said it wasn't likely,
yet you earned a Morehouse degree.
Cuz God didn't make a mistake.
A motorcycle was forbidden
and you defiantly bought one anyway.
They advised you not to fly long distances,
so you went to work in Africa.
You were sure to have a lucrative career at Jet magazine,
but you became a teacher.
You said God wouldn't make a mistake.
While your grandfather only lived
until you were eleven years old,
he taught you how to be a man.
Repeating history, as if it were written,
you passed it all on to your son.
In his first ten years, he gained everything he needs
to be the man you were and more.
Because God makes no mistakes.
Although we will miss you,
and feel an emptiness in your absence,
your spirit fills our hearts.
You dared to live life unrestricted
loving and living abundantly.
You have taught us all that
life is to be lived to the fullest,
and to not fear the end.
And we believe you that God made no mistake.

Through my recovery, my life's purpose was becoming clearer. Helping others build their resilience by sharing my experience gave purpose to my pain. About six months after Scott passed away, the National Multiple Sclerosis Society asked me to deliver a workshop to their staff. I had been a guest presenter on the topics of managing and navigating change over several previous years. However, as a new widow, I had a deeper perspective on change and a more profound understanding of the importance of resilience in moving through tough experiences.

I wanted to share my personal journey while maintaining the professionalism they expected from me. I feared I'd break down if I talked in too much detail about my loss. Before the workshop, I prayed for discernment to provide the personal perspective that would inspire without disclosing anything I might later regret.

When I went before the class, I heard Scott's voice say in my mind, "Be authentic, be vulnerable, be yourself." That is when I promised myself, and Scott, that I would teach and engage in resilience work with his spirit as my guide on the side.

Recovery through widowhood did not mean stopping life. It meant moving forward while reflecting on the purpose of my pain. I made meaning out of tragedy. I engaged with my strong network of sister-friends who listened to my stories and let me share my tears, joy, and pain. Recovery included sharing, caring, connecting, and reflecting.

In their work on self-efficacy, Benight and Bandura studied how people cope with the aftermath of traumatic events, such as natural disasters. They highlighted the importance of self-efficacy in responding to and recovering from acute shocks and chronic stressors in healthy ways (Benight & Bandura, 2004).

Their research on surviving trauma showed evidence that coping self-efficacy was a vital part of the ability to recover from traumatic events. Their Trauma Coping Self-Efficacy Scale tool asked participants to rate their confidence in handling nine post-traumatic demands on a seven-point Likert scale (1 = Not at all capable, 7 = Totally capable). These items included:

1. Get my life back to normal
2. Not be critical of myself about what happened
3. Get help from others about what happened
4. Deal with unwanted memories
5. Manage my emotions related to the trauma
6. Talk about what happened without becoming overwhelmed
7. Make good decisions about my recovery
8. Stay calm when reminded of the trauma
9. Take care of my responsibilities despite the trauma

These items reflect a survivor's perceived ability to manage internal and external demands following trauma, including emotional regulation, social support, and functional recovery (Benight, et al., 2015). Their research highlights the importance of taking care of ourselves mentally, emotionally, spiritually, physically, and financially in the aftermath of a crisis. It underscores the value of the recovery phase of building resilience.

Self-Reflection Activity:
RECOVERING FROM SHIFT

For this exercise, you will examine a range of strategies you can use to recover from shifts in your life. Follow these two steps to complete this activity:

Step 1: Identify one or more shifts you have experienced or expect to happen in your life, then reflect on how it impacted you or how you expect it to impact you.

Step 2: For each shift, describe healthy and productive ways you did, or might have, recovered from that shift. Consider how you could apply the nine items from the Trauma Coping Self-Efficacy Scale.

An example is provided here for your reference.

Shifts That Happened or Are Expected to Happen and the Impact	Recovery Strategies
Example: *I lost my position due to a reorganization. My ego was bruised, I was fearful about losing my income and angry about feeling betrayed.*	*Example:* *I talked about my anger, fear, uncertainty, and pain with my mentors and friends.* *I enrolled in a PhD program and used the time to work on myself.* *I identified the positive ways I could use this experience to better my life.*
Shifts That Happened or Are Expected to Happen and the Impact	Recovery Strategies

Summary

Our lived experiences give us perspective on ourselves, the world around us, and the people in our lives. The ups and downs of life prepare us for what is ahead and build our individual resilience.

In the *Handbook of Posttraumatic Growth: Research and Practice*, Calhoun and Tedeschi describe the growth that can happen when a person experiences a difficulty that "shakes their world." While they distinguish post-traumatic growth (PTG) from resilience, asserting that resilience does not always lead to growth, they do recognize that it is a key ingredient in the ability to grow from challenges. They also explain that we should not dismiss or disregard the pain associated with adverse events (Calhoun & Tedeschi, 2006).

"Negative events tend to produce, for most persons, consequences that are negative" (p. 4). That said, the results of their research are both impressive and inspirational. They shared that "for many persons, the encounter with very negative events can also produce positive psychological change" (p. 4). They describe five key positive results that can emerge after adversity.

The first positive outcome is a **greater sense of personal strength**. Maybe you've looked back on a difficult situation and said to yourself, "Wow, I can't believe I got through that. I am much stronger than I thought I was!" I felt that way after escaping a violent relationship that went on way too long. I stayed in it because I felt powerless. Yet when I finally mustered the courage to leave, I realized that I'd had the strength to leave all along. I also later learned that I deserved to have a loving relationship with an emotionally healthy person. It was a painful lesson (both physically and emotionally), but I showed myself how strong I could be.

The second positive outcome is **developing the ability to see the silver linings** inside dark clouds of difficulty. Calhoun and Tedeschi call this "the ability to see new possibilities." The hardest part of change (especially a traumatic change) is the uncertainty and unfamiliarity of what is to come next. We want to know, or even control, what is around the corner. That predictability gives us a sense of safety and security. Post-traumatic growth research showed that uncertainty can unlock new opportunities people would not have otherwise considered when they were in a comfortable state.

The third benefit is **finding interactions with others more meaningful**. After my husband died, I had a new appreciation for relationships with family members and others around me in general. It put things in perspective. Things that annoyed me before were no longer important. When you realize how short and fragile life really is, you recognize that any interaction with a loved one could be the last, so you must make it count.

The fourth blessing is a **deeper appreciation for life**. That seems obvious, but many of us do not stop to think every day that we are just glad to be alive. When you experience loss or a brush with your own mortality, it awakens you to the reality that not one more day is guaranteed. Adversities have offered me the chance to reevaluate my life's balance and shown me that I need to spend less time developing what **I do** and what **I have**, and invest more in who **I am**. It makes me ask myself, "Am I truly living in my purpose? How do I want to be remembered when I leave this Earth?"

Finally, Calhoun and Tedeschi describe how adversity can lead to a **greater connection to our higher power**, or our spiritual center, and elevate our awareness about the need to be mindful. Living with intention, taking time for meditation, and keeping your mind in the present moment are all actions that build resilience. Challenges are often exclamatory reminders that you need to take a pause to pray, reflect, and regenerate your spirit. Over the past ten years, I have learned that prayer and meditation are important for me not only when things are hard, but also during calm and joyful times.

3

Values Can Guide You Through Life's Shifts

Do you rely on Google Maps, Waze, or another GPS app to get where you want to go? Navigation guidance helps us stay on the right course and avoid getting lost. Even when we know where we are going, it helps to have additional guidance to avoid hazards and find better pathways.

Sometimes, we need a reminder about our intended destination. It is easy to get distracted by things around us and even the thoughts in our heads. Have you ever been driving on a familiar route and suddenly asked yourself, "Where the heck am I going?" You are not alone. Many of us experience this in both driving and in life.

As you navigate a shift, your values can guide you through life's unpredictable twists and turns. They can serve as your internal GPS to remind you where you want to go, why you want to go there, and the best routes to take. Values nudge you back onto the right route if you find yourself going astray. I have found four values most important for navigating the ups and downs of life. They follow the first four letters of the alphabet: authenticity, balance, clarity, and discipline.

Navigation Value 1: Authenticity

The Merriam-Webster dictionary defines authenticity as "being true to one's own personality, spirit, or character." The ups and downs have taught me the importance of authenticity in creating a joyous life. When things get tough, you might be tempted to sacrifice authenticity for acceptance, security, predictability, and connection. Conformity is often expected for success in a society deeply entrenched in predefined ways of interacting. When a life shift unseats you from your place of comfort, authenticity can help you find your true place in this world.

Living authentically is experiencing life with alignment between your core values and the actions you take. It is freedom to be who you are at your core and honor your identity while succeeding in a diverse society.

Many of us are pressured, or even rewarded, to live in a way that makes others comfortable at the expense of truth to ourselves. When you are not living authentically, you may experience cognitive dissonance, an internal conflict between how you behave and what you believe. That internal conflict can be painful and lead to self-condemnation. At the same time, living authentically may require taking risks or making sacrifices.

When I worked as a human resources manager in a manufacturing plant, I experienced daily challenges as one of few women at the company and the only Latina. I was often involved in decisions that impacted people's employment and considered myself to be the voice of compassion, empathy, and inclusion. Some of my colleagues were clearly uncomfortable when I questioned their decisions. There were times when they left me out of conversations relevant to my job because they didn't want to hear my point of view. I had to make a daily choice: Either stand up for what I believed in or be silent so others could be comfortable. I had to master the art of diplomacy; to be 100 percent straightforward without insulting or disrespecting those who viewed things differently than I did.

Many times, I wondered if I was too authentic. However, fifteen years later, I received a surprising message from Jack, a plant manager I worked with on some very challenging situations:

"Hello, I was thinking of you today regarding the lessons I learned working with you, building a team of people from diverse backgrounds. It was a privilege, and I hope you are well."

I was honored and humbled to receive this message from him. Jack and I had many spirited conversations over the two years we worked together. There were tough decisions that had to be made, as well as complex people issues to navigate. I brought my authentic and loving spirit. As a result, he did not feel anger or hostility toward or from me, and the experience enriched both of us.

Being accepted by others is an important human need that is not exclusive from our need for authenticity. You can have both. During times of unplanned change, crisis, or chaos, your authenticity can be challenged. You might be tempted to waive your values or put them aside—especially if your survival is on the line. Yet you pay a price when you suppress your authentic self. It can bankrupt your spirit in this lifetime and diminish the value of the legacy you leave for others. The art of authenticity lies in being both truthful and strategic, avoiding unnecessary risks to yourself and those you care about while not compromising who you are at your core.

Navigation Value 2: Balance

Living in balance involves investing the right proportions of time and energy in the various aspects of life. It is easy to become deeply drawn into career needs at the expense of family life. At the same time, many people can be pulled into family life at the expense of their physical and emotional well-being.

Having balance as a value allows you to put things into their proper perspective and prominence. Your professional, social, financial, physical, and spiritual dimensions do not always need to be equally weighted. However, finding the right balance across these dimensions is key.

When I was a global consultant, I spent about 80 percent of my time traveling. It was a wonderfully enriching experience as I worked on projects that took me to Israel, Argentina, Chile, the United Kingdom, Spain, Ireland, El Salvador, Uruguay, Peru, and Canada. Scott was a great partner, serving as our young son's full-time care provider as I traveled. As with most Big Four consulting firms, we were expected to work around the clock, even pulling all-nighters if that was needed to deliver value to our clients.

One Friday afternoon, when I was home from traveling, I joined Scott for our son's second-grade parent-teacher conference. During the discussion, his teacher, Meagan, raised a concern.

"I must tell you something that Sage asked me," she said. "He said, 'Will you be my mommy, because mine is never home?'"

The words stung, but I knew Sage was right: My life was out of balance. The challenge was that getting it into balance would have required me to make a professional shift because traveling was a job requirement. That was a change I was not ready to make—until the greatest loss of my life forced it.

For another two years, I stayed on the road. I tucked my little boy in at night by videoconference and caught up on hugs during the fast-moving weekends. Scott continued to hold things down at home so I could put all my energy into my work. I thought delegating meant I was balancing. However, when Scott died, I didn't have a crutch to lean on anymore. In the first weeks of school after Scott's death, I got a call from Sage's principal:

"Is someone coming to pick Sage up from carpool? He has been sitting on the curb for nearly an hour."

Oh my goodness! I forgot all about my own child! The imbalance was really in my face now, and I had to make a choice. I'd always counted on Scott to be the primary parent, and now it was just me. Better balance was long overdue. But now it was inescapable.

"Find a career that allows better balance or abandon your child while he is grieving," I said, stating the options out loud to myself. It was an easy choice.

For six months, I searched for a new position, hoping to land a rewarding career with a local company where I would not be required to travel. I wanted to use my skills and my hard-earned degrees. I didn't want to lose income, especially since I was a single parent once again. I tapped into my spiritual connection and went into prayer, asking my Higher Power to show me the way. I knew I would have to be patient and open to the plan **set out** for me.

Not long after I began to pray in earnest, I received an email newsletter from a recruiting company in my spam inbox. Even though it wasn't addressed directly to me, something told me to follow the link. There, in just two clicks, was a position description that looked as if it had been written specifically for me:

Looking for a professional with the following qualifications:

- ☑ *PhD - check!*

- ☑ *Management consulting experience - check!*

- ☑ *Government or higher education experience - check!*

- ☑ *Experience managing change - double check!*

From the first interview, I knew this was the perfect place for me. After the first six months of working there, my sweet little boy said to me, "Mommy, I really feel like I know you now. Maybe there is one good thing that happened after losing Daddy." He enjoyed attending summer camps on the college campus where I now work. The loss, uncertainty, and change gave me a better balance than I was willing to give myself.

Navigation Value 3: Clarity

Clarity is like the headlights of your life that let you see what is in front of you. During dark and stormy times, you might need to use your high beams to illuminate the road ahead. As you face challenges, clarity is essential. It increases the likelihood that you will see things logically and rationally as they really are, and not through the lenses of your own darkest imagination.

I spent much of my early adulthood with clouded vision. I could not see the truth about the world around me because I struggled to see the truth about myself. That led me into harmful relationships, and it was part of the reason I stayed with an abusive man for so long. I did not believe I was worthy of a loving and respectful relationship. I had internalized the direct and indirect messages that permeated my childhood. Others told me I did not deserve respect, and I believed them. When we see ourselves as inferior, and our self-esteem is low, we are easily manipulated.

My low self-esteem made me an easy target for predatory actors. Not long after breaking free from the destructive cycle of the first abusive relationship, I became involved with a man named Tom. He was tall and slender, and he walked with a cool swagger that exuded confidence. He told me he was an undercover agent for a federal agency. He had a badge and a uniform, and he told me elaborate stories about how he was investigating crime rings. I was looking for a protector, so I ate up every morsel he was dishing out.

In my excitement, I reached out to my friend Jeffrey, whom I had met through a federal training program. I told him all about Tom.

"You guys might know each other," I said, "since you are both in federal law enforcement." I envisioned building a life with Tom, even though I just met him.

My trust deepened over the next few weeks until I got a visit from Jeffrey at work.

"Can you come outside for a minute, Sonia?" he asked. His expression was stern. I followed him to his car, where he handed me a two-by-two-inch photo. It was Tom!

"What is this?" I asked. But I already knew the answer.

"It is a mug shot," he replied. "He was recently released from prison for impersonating a federal officer."

I sat speechless in the passenger seat of his unmarked police car, mouth gaping open. How could I be so naïve? I had been so afraid of my former abuser that I believed it all. I was running away from someone bad, rather than running toward someone good.

Jeffrey and I went back into the office and used my boss's cubicle to have a private call with the special agent-in-charge. His name was John. Jeffrey asked me to tell John everything about Tom. I told him how he would go out with his gun, badge, and uniform to supposedly catch bad guys in the middle of the night.

Later that night, the real federal agents Jeffrey and John, came by my apartment to get an official statement. John sat down, looked right into my eyes, and said, "I don't know how you got yourself into a situation like this. You seem like a smart young lady, but this was a bad decision. You can do much better than a guy like that. We will let him know that he better never bother you again, but you must make better choices."

He was right.

John checked in on me over the next few weeks to make sure Tom didn't try to retaliate. Through these check-in calls, he challenged me to see my potential and tap into the good parts of myself that I had been unable to see.

For the next ten years, John mentored me like a caring big brother. He introduced me to people who could help me grow professionally and opened my eyes to possibilities for my life I had never imagined. I will never forget the time he said to me, "I can see you getting your Ph.D. someday." That seemed far-fetched, as I was still living in the housing projects and struggling from paycheck to paycheck. I didn't even have an associate degree!

Yet through his vision for me, I was able to see the road ahead so much more clearly. He taught me to dream about my future and see things for what they could be.

Nearly three decades after meeting John, the cop-turned-mentor who changed the trajectory of my life, I went in search of him. We had lost contact after I married Scott. I found him via Facebook and learned that he had experienced a terrible fall that left him unable to walk, speak, or even hold his head up straight. I sent him a video message that his brother played for him. I told him how his mentorship changed my life and that I owed my success to the fact that he showed me good in myself. A few months later, I received this message from his brother:

> *"I have some sad news. Johnny passed away yesterday. His body had been ravaged, and over time, it just could not continue to fight all the complications that come with being a quadriplegic. I'm sure you know how he felt about you. And when you gave those heartfelt words about how he encouraged and helped you, I don't believe you know how much you helped him. You see, Johnny became very cynical and negative in the last few years of his career and prior to his accident. It happens to a lot of cops because they forget to balance their career with outside interests that have nothing to do with police work. They forget to look for the good people. Anyway, whenever he would go off on a negative tangent about how shitty people are and that their destiny and lot in life are fixed, I would bring him back to reality by mentioning your name ... Then he'd smile. Thank you, Dr. Alvarez, for all you did to help my brother."*

In Buddhist teachings, there is a concept of ten "worlds," or spiritual realms, that describe our states of existence. These worlds are along a continuum ranging from Hell (the state of immense suffering) to Buddhahood (joy, peace, and liberation from suffering). Buddhists believe we can break free from the "lower life states" through conscious attention to our thoughts and actions. Through intentionality and clarity, we can "transcend illusion and manifest enlightenment" (Soka Gakkai International). Whatever your spiritual beliefs, engaging in the regular practice of meditation and reflection can sharpen your clarity on the world to help you better understand your place in it.

Clarity occurs when your needs, desires, passions, interests, and strengths come together with your purpose. When change happens to you, things may become unclear about where you should go next. Having clarity of your vision for the bigger picture allows you to pivot to new ways of living your purpose. Clarity around what you want in life supports your ability to maintain authenticity and balance. Being clear about what you deserve and need helps you stay on the right track, especially when there are bumps in the road.

Navigation Value 4: Discipline

Living with discipline involves aligning day-to-day habits with what you want to achieve. So often, we undermine our own progress by engaging in patterns of behavior that are inconsistent with our ambitions. Discipline is about following through on your commitments to yourself—both in what you need to start doing and what you should stop doing. This is particularly important during a time of loss, uncertainty, or change, when fear and anxiety can cause you to grasp for comfort.

Discipline as a guiding principle compels you to challenge yourself and how you cope with adversity. Are you grasping for what comforts you momentarily but will harm you in the long term? It takes a great deal of discipline to stop behaviors that have become habits. Many of us have been programmed to act against our own self-interest. We have been conditioned by social norms that have been engineered to bind us.

One of my goals is to be financially ready for unplanned change. I know that it is important to have at least six months of my salary saved in a cash emergency fund. But then there is Amazon! It is so easy to act on an impulse by simply opening the app. I don't even have to log in! Achieving my financial independence goal requires that I have discipline to stop unplanned spending and be more aggressive with savings. To eliminate temptation, I canceled my Amazon subscription. To make saving automatic, I enrolled in a payroll deduction savings program at work. These two actions set up parameters for self-discipline that reduce the chance that I will sabotage my own financial goals.

I learned an important lesson about discipline when I was struck from behind by a distracted driver in 2017. My son Sage and I were sitting at a stop sign when WHAM! I felt the lower half of my body shift to the left. The car was totaled, and my spine was damaged. Sage was shaken but thankfully uninjured. After two years of excruciating pain, I had spinal surgery, where they implanted a titanium cage secured with four screws between two of my vertebrae.

During the recovery from surgery, I received a monetary settlement from the other driver's insurance company. It was a sizable amount but could have been quickly spent on frivolous things. It was large enough for me to invest and multiply the value, but small enough that it could evaporate quickly with little to show for it later if I wasn't careful. I told myself I needed to spend the money on something that would last as long as the pain—which was for the rest of my life. I exercised discipline and invested the funds in real estate. I used the money to make a meaningful down payment on a beautiful lake home, where I plan to retire. In the first five years of owning this property, it doubled in value. That was the payoff of letting discipline lead my decision-making.

I have also been learning about discipline over the past three years by working through the twelve steps of Nar-Anon. It is a community support program for those who have loved ones suffering from the disease of addiction. The program teaches how discipline can be life-saving. I have learned that the best thing I can do for a person who is harming themselves with the compulsive use of drugs is to not rescue them.

It is counterintuitive to refrain from helping someone you love, but when you enable them, you impede them from taking ownership of their own life. It takes discipline to get out of their way and let them find their own path to recovery.

"Clean up your own side of the street" is a slogan I learned that helps you maintain the discipline to address your own defects of character (I sure do have many of them), rather than trying to get others to address theirs.

In the face of adversity, we tend to grasp for things that are familiar, convenient, and comfortable. Daily behaviors and practices, and how we spend our time and resources, must be aligned with things that are helpful to our growth and what we want to accomplish. I often told my sons that "maturity is the distance you put between stimulus and response."

Discipline is about restraining yourself from doing things that are counterproductive to your own best interests. Like resistance strength training, you can build muscle through resistance and restraint. Discipline helps you gain physical, emotional, financial, and spiritual strength and holds you accountable for living the life you desire, especially during times of loss, uncertainty, change, and dealing with your kinfolk.

Summary

Life shifts can compel you to make decisions at some of the most difficult times of your life. Your values can guide you through these challenging decisions so you can avoid regret.

In my life's journey, I have learned from two kinds of regrets. First, regretting doing something I wish I had **not** done, and second, regretting not doing something I wish I **had** done. Invariably, using my values as a guide has helped me avoid both kinds of regrets. More importantly, values have helped me move forward on a path of positive mental, physical, and emotional well-being as I navigated difficulties.

Values as your guideposts can help you prepare for, respond to, and recover from loss, uncertainty, change, and issues with kinfolk. As you take ownership of your life's shifts, you may find authenticity, balance, clarity, and discipline helpful. Consider what other values you will apply in your life. How will you demonstrate those values? How will you know when your life is aligned with them?

Self-Reflection Activity:
SETTING YOUR VALUES

For this exercise, you will set parameters to help you navigate life's winding road. Consider how you set the parameters on your GPS before you take a trip. Do you want to avoid certain conditions or roadways? Follow these two steps to complete this activity:

Step 1: *Identify the values that are important to you. Think of the navigation guidance you will need to stay on the right path as you encounter loss, uncertainty, change, and challenges with kinfolk.*

Step 2: *For each value, provide some examples of the practices and behaviors that you will demonstrate consistently to model that value. Challenge yourself to think of how you would test your values when you are under stress or duress.*

Here's one example to help you get started.

Value: What GPS guidance does your life need?	**Behaviors/Actions:** What behaviors and practices will you consistently demonstrate when you are living this value?
Example: *Following through on commitments to myself and others.*	☞ *Avoid overcommitting or agreeing to do things to please or appease others.* ☞ *Learn to say no.* ☞ *Get better organized and track commitments to completion.* ☞ *Establish and stick to a balanced schedule.*
Value: What GPS guidance does your life need?	**Behaviors/Actions:** What behaviors and practices will you consistently demonstrate when you are living this value?

4

Defining Your Destination

Knowing where you want to go, and why, can help you stay on the right track as you navigate the twists and turns of life. Both the **where** and the **why** can serve as fuel to power you through the ups and downs. Defining your purpose and vision can give you the energy you need to keep going and be a source of light to illuminate the frightening, unclear, and changing path ahead. Just as values give you the guidance to stay on your path, defining your purpose and vision will keep you focused on where you want to go and why.

The Power of Purpose

Having a clear sense of purpose is helpful when you're maneuvering through any unexpected shift. Just as if you were taking a coast-to-coast road trip, you might need to adjust your planned route based on road conditions. But that will not change **why** you are taking the trip. When I experienced job loss, widowhood, spinal injury, and the serious health conditions of people I love deeply, I found myself having to revisit my **why**. I had many questions about my life:

- ☞ What will make my life worthwhile?

- ☞ What difference do I want to make?

- ☞ What are my gifts, and how should I use them?

Things that shake us and disrupt our lives have a way of calling us to take stock of our purpose. In times of crisis, chaos, or unexpected change, you may need to revisit your mission and adapt to new circumstances. That doesn't change the **why** of your life, but it may just shift **how** you pursue it.

My long-time friend Daphyne, a compassionate woman with a love for people across cultures, was living in New Orleans when Hurricane Katrina hit. Her home and workplace were both destroyed. She had been working for a local nonprofit that could not afford to rebuild, and she was out of a job. Contemplating her next move, she looked deeply into her passions, interests, and strengths to decide what to do next. She returned to her Midwest hometown to regroup. There, she drew upon her Peace Corps, public health, and nonprofit experience to pursue an international aid assignment in Africa. She followed her mission to help vulnerable people and went to work delivering life-saving public health programs. She ventured a long way from New Orleans but was no less aligned in delivering her mission.

Many people search for purpose their whole life. Countless books have been written on the subject, and defining it is often a difficult thing to do. You might find yourself living in service of what others want for your life. You might simply be fulfilling what you stumbled into out of necessity, convenience, or opportunity. There is no shame in being in that place. But when life's plans fall apart, it's important to have a point to pivot from.

In *Man's Search for Meaning*, Holocaust survivor Viktor Frankl eloquently expresses that, "One should not search for an abstract meaning of life. Everyone has his [or her] specific vocation or mission in life to carry out a concrete assignment which demands fulfillment" (Frankl, 2006, p. 109).

Buddhism taught me to find answers through a daily practice of meditation and a life centered around peaceful coexistence. In *Fundamentals of Buddhism*, Yasuji Kirimura writes,

> *If people understand the true entity of their lives, they can live wisely and deal with any situation effectively. Such enlightenment manifests itself as inexhaustible wisdom which illuminates every aspect of one's own existence and the society in which one lives (Kirimura, 1993, p. 15).*

Finding your mission requires openness to connect with your inner spirit and the energy of the world around you. Creating a stillness will allow you to listen to your life, the universe, or a Higher Power (whatever approach works best for you) to find inner clarity. You can achieve this through meditation, reflection, or prayer (even if you do not believe in a Higher Power).

Your statement of your purpose (or mission) can evolve as you develop greater clarity about your strengths, interests, passions, and gifts. Shifts happen both in the world **around** you and **within** you. As you prepare to develop your mission statement, start simple:

- What do you **like** to do?

- What are you **good** at?

- What brings you **joy** and a **sense of pride**?

- If you could make a living doing something you would do for free anyway, what would it be?

Before you can think about deeper questions—such as Why have you been given life?—think about it at a general level:

- What contributions do you dream about making in the world?

- How do you want to be remembered after you leave this Earth?

A friend who owns a moving services company shared his mission with me: "Helping people transition from one place to another while making good money and giving others a chance to work and feed their families too." While this mission statement is focused on his business, it also includes his passion for helping others and adding value to the broader society.

Early in my career, I actively pursued working in human resources. I studied hard for seven long years to earn my bachelor's degree in three focus areas (human resources management, philosophy, and political science) then pursued graduate education in human development and organizational studies. I felt strongly that my purpose was to **create positive working environments and help people be their best at work**. I poured my time and energy into carrying out that mission at work and by volunteering in the community. I got a job working as an HR manager. All of it aligned with what I felt was my core mission.

As I learned more about myself and gained new insights through my experiences with job loss and widowhood, I adjusted my mission. I revised it to acknowledge my new experiences, perspectives, and insights. My new mission statement is "To demonstrate faith, hope, and resilience by effectively preparing for, adapting to, and thriving through change." As my life has evolved and I've gained new experiences, my understanding of the legacy I want to leave has sharpened. Loss, uncertainty, change, and challenges with kinfolk have helped me to clarify my purpose.

Self-Reflection Activity:
DRAFTING YOUR MISSION

For this activity, you will reflect on some key questions about your purpose. Find a quiet space free from distractions where your attention to this activity will not compete with your phone, family, friends, or work. Find a place where you can be with just you and your source of inspiration.

Defining your authentic purpose might be one of the hardest things you have considered. The questions here are designed to help you think about your experiences, interests, passions, and strengths. As you consider each question, your purpose statement should begin to take shape. Schedule at least thirty minutes of focused time to contemplate each question and another thirty minutes to summarize. Plan as many sessions as needed to complete the questions, then go back and review them with a fresh mind at another time. Remember, this is iterative. You will keep refining it throughout life. It does not need to be perfect, and it is not a lifetime commitment to do one specific thing. It is about setting a direction to pursue your purpose, recognizing that it may shift as your life does.

Use the space on the following pages to write your thoughts about the following three question sets:

1. **What do you enjoy the most?** Think of the most pleasant and enjoyable times of your life. They can be experiences you have had at work, in your social life, or alone. What were you doing? How were you feeling? What was the impact?

2. **What are you good at?** What are your strengths? Brainstorm a list of the situations when you have been at your best and felt natural and confident about

what you were doing. Where were you? Who were you around? What and who were you doing it for? What was the impact?

3. **Where have you added real, meaningful value?** Brainstorm a list of situations when you felt that you did something that added real value. Where have you done the most good? What and who were you doing it for?

4. **Summarize:** After you have answered these three question sets, look for common themes. What patterns do you notice? Where have you found the greatest joys?

The Value of Vision

Visioning is a process of **defining your desired life state**. That vision can be both **for today (the now) and tomorrow (the future)**. Unlike goal setting, visioning keeps your view on the big picture. It is the quality of life you aspire to. This is not a fixed view of the future, but the conditions that you want to create as you harness your self-efficacy and internal locus of control.

Unexpected shifts can significantly disrupt your plans. So, you must recognize that vision is a fluid view of the life you are living today and the days ahead of you. You can be agile and give yourself freedom to adjust your vision according to shifts in your life circumstances.

Understanding what joy means can give you clarity as you move through change. Envisioning your ideal life state through the lens of joy can show you what you really need and want for your life.

Oftentimes, plans are dependent, and interdependent, on other people and specific circumstances (such as plans with loved ones or plans in a particular job or employment environment). The quality of your lived experience is interconnected with others, and you must recognize that these dependencies have the potential to change. Creating a life of astounding joys requires a vision that you can fulfill without complete dependency on others.

When I got married, my vision relied heavily on Scott's presence and maintaining the healthy relationship we enjoyed. After he died, my vision shifted to become dependent on my role as a mother. Now that my children are adults, I need a new vision about **my life**—independent of anyone else. My vision for the ideal life was also highly dependent on my employment situation. While that remains an important part of my life, I know my vision needs greater balance.

I have learned along the way that creating a life vision should provide a balanced view that includes at least five dimensions, as shown in the diagram on the following page:

5 Dimensions of a RESILIENT LIFE

1

Spiritual:

Centering your life in a way that anchors your heart and soul. Beyond worship practices or the doctrine you believe in, it is about YOUR spirit and your connection to sources of energy and clarity.

2

Physical

Taking care of your body from the inside out. Including your organs, muscles, systems, fluids, bones, and skin – every part of your anatomy.

3

Professional

Living your mission through your studies or your work. It's not just about a job or a major, but how you use your gifts and the contributions you make.

4

Social

Life outside of work or school. Your ideal family, community, and societal experiences. Healthy relationships with people in your life.

5

Financial

Beyond income, your total wealth (what you own and what you owe). Maintaining a healthy quality of life while earning a living.

Figure 6. Five Vision Elements

A balanced vision considers five elements of life:

1. **Spiritual**: This is the centering force in your life that anchors your heart and soul. This is not just about worship or doctrine. It is about YOUR spirit and the reality you envision for the spiritual part of your life. How and where do you desire to engage your spiritual energy? What does peace look like for you?

2. **Physical**: Imagine your ideal physical self in terms of every aspect of your being. Think about your body from the inside out—your organs, your systems, your fluids, your bones, your skin, and every other part of your anatomy. In your desired state, how will you feel, function, and look?

3. **Professional/Academic**: In your career, imagine your best life when you are truly living your mission. Your professional aspect is not just about a job. It is how and where you spend your time in your studies, vocation, and industrious contributions. What is your ideal professional reality or academic success? How is it aligned with your purpose?

4. **Social**: This aspect is about your interactions with others and includes your ideal family, community, and societal experiences. What social reality do you desire that is aligned with your mission? As you envision your relationships with yourself and others, what do you hope for the future?

5. **Financial**: Your financial aspect is not only about income. It is about total wealth, including what you own and what you owe. It is about the quality of life you want to create with your financial resources. What is your ideal financial situation? How do you want to experience the financial art of your life, considering your mission?

Vision Example

Each person's vision for their future is unique and specific to their mission. Using the mission statement example shown earlier—**"To demonstrate faith, hope, and resilience by effectively preparing for, adapting to, and thriving through change"**—I created these vision statements for the five dimensions of my life:

- ☞ **Spiritual**: I envision unwavering faith that my Creator has a plan for me and those I love so that I can release my worries about things that are outside my control.

- ☞ **Physical**: I picture entering my later years healthy and energetic, free from pain or chronic illness, and continuing to have the energy, strength, and endurance to take care of myself.

- ☞ **Financial**: I want to maintain my current high quality of living even if I experience a major unexpected expense or loss of income. My vision is to be working only when and where I want after I turn sixty.

- ☞ **Social**: I desire connection with people who share my values, care for me as a person, and are trustworthy. My social vision is that I will have healthy, reciprocal, respectful relationships with friends and family who value me the way I do them.

- ☞ **Professional**: I aspire to work on projects that compensate me well and benefit others at the same time. My aim is for others to benefit from the lessons, hardships, and failures I have experienced as I share knowledge through leading, mentoring, writing, and teaching.

As I reviewed each of these five dimensions, I created a synthesized vision statement that ties together the most important elements of my desired reality—for today and for my future. My overall vision for my life, aligned with my mission, is

> **66 To live a healthy, simple, focused, and flexible life that empowers and inspires others to thrive through life's ups and downs. 99**

Your vision should guide your decisions and establish your priorities. Each vision element will require that you set boundaries while maintaining habits that are aligned with your ambitions. This is where your values are crucial. By declaring your vision, you can set an intention to create the life you envision, guided by your core values.

Self-Reflection Activity:
DEFINING YOUR VISION

In a quiet place, contemplate the following questions about your ideal life state for each of the five dimensions. Write down your thoughts on each question in the space provided. Start with your mission statement (even if it is a draft) and then answer the visioning questions in the spaces provided:

Mission Statement:

Visioning Questions:

1. **Spiritual:** Describe the ideal relationship with your Higher Power and/or your spiritual center.

    ☞ What is the ideal reality for the spiritual aspect of your life?

    ☞ Is there a difference between the ideal and your reality now? If so, what do you want to be different?

2. **Physical:** Envision your ideal physical state, both inside your body and what the world can see.

    ☞ In the ideal reality, what do you want for the physical aspect of your life?

    ☞ Is there a difference between the ideal and your actual reality now? If so, what do you want to be different?

3. **Professional/Academic:** Consider the lasting impact you want to leave through your work or studies.

    ☞ In the ideal reality, what do you want for your professional or academic life?

    ☞ Is there a difference between the ideal and your actual reality now? If so, what do you want to be different?

4. **Social:** Imagine the relationships you desire to have with others.

    ☞ In the ideal reality, what do you want for the social aspect of your life?

    ☞ Is there a difference between the ideal and your actual reality now? If so, what do you want to be different?

5. **Financial:** Think not only about possessions and accumulation of wealth, but your intention for how you want to live.

- ☞ In the ideal reality, what do you want for the financial part of your life?

- ☞ Is there a difference between the ideal and your actual reality now? If so, what do you want to be different?

6. **Summarize**

- ☞ Do you see any patterns?

- ☞ Where are you already aligned between your vision of your ideal life state and what you are experiencing today?

- ☞ Where will you strengthen your life to be more consistent with your aspirations?

Summary

As you contemplate the life you want to create, be cautious that you don't lose sight of the present. Take stock of where you are now, what you know today, who you love, and who loves you. I have learned this lesson the hard way. My bias toward preparing for the future has often caused me to miss the value of the present moment. At times, I have been so worried about where I am going that I missed the beauty of the journey to get there.

In *The Power of Now*, Ekhart Tolle writes about how often we get caught up in our heads, ruminating about the past or fretting about the future. He describes how we miss the joy of the present: "This incessant mental noise prevents us from finding that realm of inner stillness that is inseparable from being" (Tolle, 2004, p. 15).

One sunny, clear afternoon, I was driving to an event where I was to accept a community service award from the Kappa Alpha Psi fraternity. I prepared a short acceptance speech and was nervous. My mind was churning about what I would say, how I would say it, and who would be in the audience. My mind wandered away from the task at hand—driving! I blew right through a red light and WHAM! My car was T-boned, and I was dumbfounded. As I lay on the gurney in the back of the ambulance, the sirens whirling, I remembered a quote someone shared with me: "While it's good to have an end to journey toward, it's the journey that counts in the end."

Obsessing about the future isn't the only challenge many of us face as we clarify our vision. It is easy to get stuck in what happened in the past. Looking through life's rearview mirror can be instructive, but you can't move forward if you are always looking backward. Looking through the windshield is not only about anticipating the destination, but also about being aware of your present location. The rearview mirror is much smaller than the windshield for a reason! Living a full life requires learning from the past, living in the present, and preparing for the future.

Practicing mindfulness can quiet anxieties about tomorrow and free you from the pain of your past. Thich Nhất Hạnh, a renowned Buddhist monk, scholar, teacher, and author, offers insights to help us stay connected to the present in *Living Buddha, Living Christ.* He presents an easy exercise you can practice anywhere:

"Breathing in, I calm my body. Breathing out, I smile. Dwelling in the present moment. I know this is a wonderful moment" (Nhất Hạnh, 1997, p. 21).

PART 2

Fifteen Lessons for Building Resilience

5

Introducing the Resilience FIRST Model™

In the fall of 2019, I developed a college-level course called Strategies for Building Resilience: Growing Through What We Are Going Through with my colleague Dr. Joi Alexander, director of the Wellness Empowerment Center. Together, we created a five-week program for undergraduate and graduate students to equip them with skills they could use to deal with acute shocks and chronic stressors of life. We wanted to equip students with psychological and behavioral tools for navigating challenges during and beyond their college careers. We launched the course in the spring of 2020, just before the start of the global pandemic. The last day of our ten-session course fell on March 12, 2020, the day before the world went into lockdown.

Since then, we have taught eighteen cohorts of this course, continuing to refine and strengthen it as we gained new insights. I have also been commissioned to write and speak on this topic for a range of professional publications and conferences. Through these reflective and interactive experiences, and my own personal journey, I developed the Resilience FIRST Model™ in 2022.

The model represents the culmination of what I learned through my experiences, as well as by reading, researching, teaching, and engaging with others on these topics. It now serves as the framework for my teaching in the classroom, in professional workshops, and in my coaching practice.

Grounded in evidence-based practices, the Resilience FIRST Model™ consists of five elements:

1. **F**ind Your Locus of Control

2. **I**nvestigate and Manage Your Fear

3. **R**eprogram Unhealthy Conditioning

4. **S**eek Healthy Support

5. **T**ake Time for Self-Care

Learning by Teaching

In the summer of 2025, my graduate research assistant, Lucas Provine, and I studied 120 anonymized resilience plan papers from students in eighteen cohorts between spring 2020 and spring 2025. In his analysis, Provine shared these key insights from the student reflections:

> ☞ **Adversity is a catalyst for growth:** Themes related to "lessons from adversity" underscored a cyclical relationship between experiencing challenges and building resilience. Most students perceived adversity as both inevitable and essential for personal growth, suggesting a belief that higher levels of resilience cannot be developed without exposure to significant challenges. This raises the theoretical question of whether there are limits to resilience

development in the absence of adversity and the potential benefits of educators exposing students to adversity in controlled environments.

☞ **Social support plays a central role:** Across all categories, students consistently emphasized the importance of developing and maintaining a strong social support system. They highlighted interpersonal skills—such as empathy, active listening, and effective communication—as critical. Many also expressed concerns about the future stability of their support systems in the face of graduation, relocation, and other major life transitions.

☞ **Transitional uncertainty is prevalent:** Many students described uncertainty about their post-graduation futures, citing concerns related to employment, relocation, adult responsibilities, and the ability to maintain or establish social support systems. These stressors reflect the complex interplay of logistical, emotional, and relational challenges inherent in transitioning to a new stage of life.

☞ **Strength calibration is necessary:** Students commonly mentioned that their personal strengths were also their areas of opportunity if overly expressed. For example, although flexibility was reported as a strength, being overly flexible led to undesirable outcomes.

With the intention of extending the five-week course to a full semester, I asked Provine to also provide me with advice for the longer course based on what was working well for student learning and what could be improved. His summary was instructive:

☞ **Focus on support systems:** Many students referenced the importance of establishing, maintaining, and improving their support systems and viewed them as major assets for resilience. Students would likely benefit from learning strategies and skills related to making the most of their support systems.

☞ **Bolster resilience plan assignments:** Creating a resilience plan assignment was described as beneficial, but it could be expanded upon for a full-semester course. Students could create resilience plans as a mid-semester assignment, allowing them the opportunity to test, reflect (via journaling assignments, etc.), and tweak their commitments to emphasize sustainability and continued success beyond the course.

☞ **Identify anticipated risks:** Many students reference a sense of uncertainty in their futures after graduation, such as searching for a job, working full-time, moving away from friends/family, maintaining a strong support system, managing finances, and so on. Students would likely benefit from spending time with these common concerns and being taught strategies related to these anticipated risks alongside the general strategies for resilience.

☞ **Make more time for depth and breakout discussions:** Several students wished for more time to explore each topic, so, we considered expanding on the existing topics presented in the mini-mester course. Students appreciated small group interactions with indications of wanting more of them. One said, "I really enjoyed the breakout sessions and wish we had more of those!"

In the fall of 2025, I expanded the course to a full semester, three-credit learning experience in the School of Psychology, where I deepened our focus on the shorter course content while adding more research about healing from trauma. We studied the body and mind connections in more scientific detail. I took Provine's advice and assigned the resilience plans mid-semester so students could test strategies from the FIRST model in their daily lives. I added role-play scenarios, daily small group discussions, more guest speakers to share personal testimonies, and time for open dialogue. The results were powerful. One student said,

> *The most valuable part of this course for me has been learning how to slow down and look at what I need instead of just pushing through everything. The different tools we learned, like reframing and checking in with my energy, helped me understand myself a lot better. I also really liked hearing everyone's stories and experiences because it made the class feel real and not just like another assignment. It showed me that resilience is something you build through practice and community, not something you magically have.*

It was also clear that the learning came through. Another student wrote, "Resilience is not merely about bouncing back from setbacks, but also about harnessing our strengths, embracing opportunities for growth, and adopting effective strategies to navigate life's challenges."

My intention for this book is to give you strategies to try out for yourself. Select the ones that work for you and leave the rest. As one of my students noted,

> *All of us have different takeaways from everything we learned. How everyone goes about building resilience is different, we were all given the same content but based on our lived experiences we took away different ways to apply that content to our lives which was very cool to see all the interpretations and how it will be used.*

6

Find Your Locus of Control

*"Just because we aren't in control doesn't mean that
we are powerless." — SAR*

Ou can plan and prepare for what is ahead of you, but you often have limited control over the circumstances around you. You can influence many parts of your life, yet there are some things that are just not within your control. Your only real control is over the actions you choose to take and how you deal with your emotional responses, moment to moment and day to day. You can manage your actions and emotions productively when you acknowledge what is out of your hands and what is within your influence or control.

A daily reminder about managing my locus of control is when I get on Atlanta's busy and often dangerous highway system. I cannot control whether other people are driving under the influence, distracted, or sleep-deprived. I know from experience that someone else could make a decision that destroys my life without warning. I also know that staying home for fear of someone else's driving behaviors would compromise my quality of life. I can't avoid the risk. It is always there.

However, I can control **my** awareness and ability to respond to the many risks. I can avoid being distracted, tired, or impaired.

I can minimize my own risks and try to steer away from harm others can cause.

The same can be said of many other life circumstances. You can control only how well-prepared you are, how you respond to threats, and how you recover from the impacts of negative experiences.

Buddhist philosophy teaches that the quality of life is the manifestation of actions (the karmic law of cause and effect) and is shaped through the cumulative actions taken today and in the past. Even if your karma is plagued with negativity, you can change it through consistent prayer, meditation, and positive actions. Buddhists believe that while we cannot control the life conditions we are born into, we can influence our future direction by attaining an enlightened life-state (Kirimura, 1993).

This perspective has helped me distinguish the difference between control and influence. The notion of control implies a direct relationship between my actions and the results. Influence infers that I can shape outcomes by creating a positive life force and guide a situation to my desired result, both directly and indirectly.

Another philosophy that illuminates the difference between control and influence is the notion of divine order. Christian teachings assert that God has a plan for all of us, and that the conditions of life are part of the plan of a power greater than us. A friend said to me once, "If you want God to laugh, just show him your plan." I have learned repeatedly through the circumstances of my life that even the best-laid plans are subject to change. Providing comfort through faith, Philippians 4:6-7 reads,

> *Do not be anxious about anything, but in every situation, by prayer and petition, with thanksgiving, present your requests to God. And the peace of God, which transcends all understanding, will guard your hearts and your minds in Christ Jesus (The Bible: King James Version).*

When it comes to locus of control, it is important to focus on how you are taking care of yourself. In my course, I share the H.A.L.T. technique with students: Notice when you are **h**ungry, **a**ngry, **l**onely, or **t**ired so that you can rest, regenerate, and refuel. One student noted in their resilience plan,

> *If we could all take a moment to pause and consider that our actions might be tainted by being hungry, angry, lonely, and tired then I think we would avoid a lot of bad behavior, unnecessary conflicts, and harsh self-criticism.*

While having a high internal locus of control is a key part of being resilient, we must recognize when we are taking it too far.

In *The Body Says No—The Cost of Hidden Stress*, researcher and physician Dr. Gabor Maté writes,

> *Many people may have the illusion that they are in control, only to find later that forces unknown to them were driving their decisions and behaviours for many, many years ... For some people, it is disease that finally shatters the illusion of control (Maté, 2019, p. 42).*

He explains how people who have suffered trauma often struggle with control: "What there is in a 'controlling' personality is deep anxiety ... The drive to control is not an innate trait but a coping style" (Maté, 2019, p. 136).

Our perceptions of locus of control are shaped by our lived experiences and the experiences of those around us. If you have faced minimal external challenges and few social or systemic barriers, you may be more inclined to have a higher sense of internal locus of control.

If you have directly and indirectly experienced external barriers, societal challenges, and marginalization, the notion of an internal locus of control may seem unrealistic.

Notice where you gravitate on this high/low locus of control continuum. Is your automatic reaction to stress, adversity, and change to obsess over things you don't control? If so, you might shift your energy toward the actions that will really make a difference.

Is your automatic reaction to feel defeated and give up quickly? Then you need to look at the situation through the lens of what you truly can control and just do it!

My life has taught me three important lessons about finding my locus of control:

LESSON #1

Let go of what you can't control

Think about the things that cause you anxiety, stress, and worry. Do you find that any of these things are completely outside your control? Are you worried about what other people do, say, and think? If so, you are not alone. I used to ruminate about whether people would value my contributions, appreciate my insights, or accept my ideas. Even in writing this book, self-doubt was tapping me on the shoulder. I am learning that criticism from others is a normal part of putting myself out there and taking risks. I must remind myself that I can't control what other people think, what they do, or how they receive me. However, I can control my own authenticity, put my best effort into my work, and carefully choose how to use the feedback I receive.

We do not have control over other people's thoughts and actions, even if we can try to influence them. Having a loved one who is suffering from mental illness has shown me the true experience of powerlessness. As I have learned from others who share this journey, our loved ones are in constant battle with their own thoughts and actions. As much as we—friends and family members—want to save them, healing is possible only when the person with the condition plays an active role in their own recovery. It has been hard to accept the truth, but my loved ones have a Higher Power, and it's not me.

I learned this lesson the hard way when Scott was fighting for his life in the ICU. I thought if I stayed at his bedside twenty-four seven, he would stay alive. Yet in the middle of the night, I was awakened to the realization that his heart had stopped. After I searched for his nurse for several minutes, a care team finally got his heart started again, but it was too late. His brain had been deprived of oxygen for so long that he would never regain normal functioning.

They asked me if I wanted them to revive him if his heart stopped again. I looked at his fragile body, barely clinging to life, and knew he would not want to live this way. It was an irrevocable decision and I had to weigh it carefully so I asked the specialists to give me the facts. What were the chances that he would ever regain the ability to interact with others? The prognosis was grim. He would likely never be able to walk, talk, feed himself, or bathe himself again. If he survived, he would need round-the-clock care. I knew that was not what he would have wanted.

I told them, "Let God do his job." They placed a bright-orange band around his soft-brown wrist that read "Allow Natural Death." I had accepted that this was a reality I couldn't control. If it was his time, there was nothing I could do to stop it.

First, I insanely believed that I had the power to control whether he lived or died. But, despite my unwavering vigilance, his suffering ended after six agonizing weeks. I had no control over the outcome, even though I was there every moment.

To let go of what you can't control, you must notice the thoughts that are affecting you negatively. Don't judge them. Just recognize that they are there and name them. It may help to write down the worry or concern and how it is impacting your quality of life. Then, ask yourself, "Is this something I can control?" If not, think about how you will release yourself from it. You may pray about it, redirect your thinking to things you can control, or write it on a piece of paper and throw it into a fire.

The important thing is to free yourself from excessive worrying about things that are outside your control.

LESSON #2

Find points of influence

As a professional strategist, I help organizations anticipate and plan for forces of influence that can impact their success. I help them set goals using a tool called a P.E.S.T.L.E. analysis, which considers multiple forces of influence on the organization: **p**olitical, **e**conomic, **s**ocial, **t**echnological, **l**egal, and **e**nvironmental. We analyze what might influence how they operate, the circumstances of the marketplace, and customer behaviors. We don't focus on trying to change those forces, for they are almost always completely outside the organization's control. We focus on preparing for expected changes and adapting to mitigate their impacts.

As a mom, I have learned that I cannot control others' actions, but I can have a positive influence through my own actions and decisions. My most regrettable actions as a parent were times when I lost control of my own actions while trying to control my sons' actions.

When Scott took me out for dinner to celebrate my birthday one year, we left the two boys (then ages twelve and fourteen) home alone for a few hours. When we got home, my younger son, David, was crouching behind the sofa with a broom in his hand.

"What are you doing?" I questioned.

"I'm scared," he replied.

"Where's your brother?"

"He left."

It was almost midnight.

"Left where?" My voice was elevating.

"I don't know. He was on the phone with someone, and then he left."

I started to panic. Scott's calm demeanor helped as I was freaking out.

"Let's just find out where he is and get him home safe," he reasoned.

I went into detective mode and found where he went. By the time I got there, he was gone. I knew that he had to work at his lifeguarding job later in the day, so I held a stakeout at the neighborhood pool where he worked. I hid behind the bushes at the entrance.

When he sauntered up through the parking lot, I jumped out at him. "Where have you been, young man?" I screamed.

Everyone turned to see what the chaos was all about. My son was shocked by my element of surprise.

"You are grounded!" I shoved his chest with both hands. I really wanted to punch him in the face.

He snickered. "What are you going to do?" he asked. "Stay home from work to keep me in the house?"

That question set me back on my heels. "No" was the answer. I couldn't make him stay in the house any more than I could stop him from going to spend the night with an older woman. But I did have control over what I would allow to happen in my house, where I paid the bills. I gave him an ultimatum: Either follow my rules or live somewhere else.

He chose the latter.

I imagined that after a week or two of living under his father's roof, he would come to see that life under my rule was much better than life in squalor without any rules. However, I failed to appreciate that a hormone-raging, rebellious, thrill-seeking teen brain would sacrifice the stability of basic needs for the reward of short-term hedonic pleasures. Regrettably, my choice to let him live with his dad, rather than keeping him close, set in motion a series of events that resulted in one heartbreak after another.

Of all the decisions I have made, this is the one I wish I could do over. It is true that I could not control my son's actions, but I could control how I responded to them. I do not wish I had tried harder to control him, but I do regret that I failed to set and maintain healthy boundaries earlier in his life. I also regret that I did not consider that some of his decision making could have been medically related. Much later in life I realized that his rebellion was rooted in resistance to the control I was trying to exert over him, combined with other mental health challenges that I did not recognize. I could have used the power of my influence to get him the care he needed, and to set healthy boundaries rather than rigid mandates.

I can't change the past, and I have learned to forgive myself. I can only take what I have learned to be a better person today and in the future. The most important thing to remember when facing challenges caused by forces outside your control is that **you are not powerless**. You can use influence to steer the situation toward a healthy outcome.

LESSON #3

Take ownership of what you can control

As discussed in the first part of this book, people who believe that they have a great deal of control over the outcomes in life are said to have a high internal locus of control. They attribute much of what happens to their actions and attribute less to external forces. Taking ownership of what they can control comes naturally.

On the other hand, people who believe that others' actions or external circumstances are the primary cause of what happens in their lives have a higher external locus of control. They often feel powerless and believe that actions to help themselves are futile. Many of us fall somewhere in the middle and recognize that our quality of life is determined by both things we can control and those we cannot.

My husband Wesley grew up in a Chicago neighborhood where healthy, natural foods, like fresh fruits and vegetables, were unaffordable and hard to find. Every corner had a store where ultra-processed foods and alcohol were plentiful, but there were no farmers' markets or grocery stores within walking distance. Chronic diseases, especially diabetes and heart disease, are a common part of his family and community experience. When he began to feel ill and was diagnosed with high blood pressure in his early forties, he just chalked it up as something that was out of his control. Several men in his immediate family died in their fifties and sixties from related illnesses. Wesley decided to just let it play out because he believed he had little control over the outcome. His perception of locus of control was shaped by his environment and early life experiences.

Eventually, he went into complete kidney failure and had to be put on dialysis. His doctor asked him, "Why didn't you take your medicine like I prescribed for you? This could have been prevented."

Wesley did not have an answer. It was just how he was programmed. But it was a wakeup call.

For several months, he underwent dialysis treatment, and the prospects of a kidney donor were woefully unlikely. However, two of his co-workers, Melinda and Charlotte, decided to seize control of what they could and set out to find him a kidney donor. They plastered his car with decals that said, "Kidney needed. Share your spare, FB@WozNeedsKidney." Within six months, Wesley received a message on Facebook from a complete stranger: "Hi, my name is Tyler and I am traveling next week to Atlanta for final testing to see if I am a match to be your kidney donor."

Wesley was stunned. He first thought it was a hoax. But after some interaction, he realized that this twenty-nine-year-old man was fully committed to saving his life.

Given his young age, the transplant center wanted Tyler to be 100 percent certain—after all, this was an irrevocable decision. They wanted him to wait for four months and set the surgery for early March 2020. We all know what happened then: The surgery was postponed due to the COVID-19 epidemic. But in May 2020, Tyler and his lovely girlfriend, Lora, flew from Arizona amid the pandemic and successfully donated his kidney.

When asked by the local news why he would give his kidney to a total stranger, Tyler responded, "Well, I have donated blood for a long time now, and this just seemed like the next thing to do." Tyler taught us so much about love, kindness, compassion, generosity, and altruism. He is a much-needed example of good in the world.

Melinda and Charlotte taught Wesley about the power of taking control over the things you can. While they could not cure his kidney disease, their actions brought Tyler to Wesley. They took control of what they could, and it resulted in a miracle.

Self-Reflection Activity:
PUTTING WORRIES INTO BUCKETS

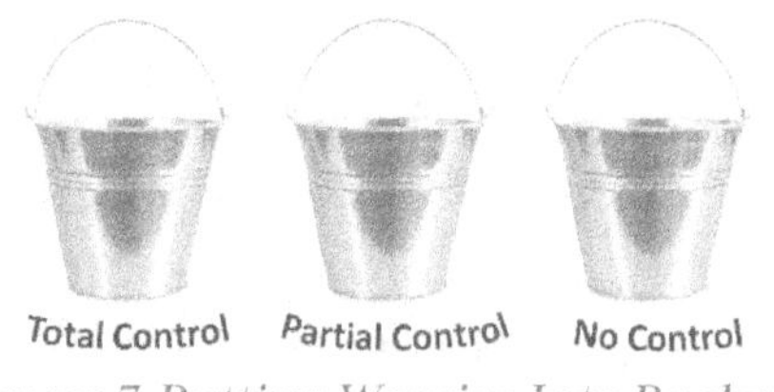

Figure 7. Putting Worries Into Buckets

Managing our worries is key to finding our locus of control. For this activity, you will follow these two steps:

Step 1: On the next page, make a list of the adversities, challenges, and changes that you worry or stress about.

Step 2: For each item on your list, assign it to one of three "buckets" as described below and answer the question for each:

- ☞ **No control:** These are completely outside your control. How will you release yourself from worrying or obsessing about them?

- ☞ **Partial control:** Here you can use influence to reduce negative impact on you. How will you influence what you can?

- ☞ **Total control:** You have full agency to shape the outcome, result, or experience. How will you take ownership and turn your worries into action?

An example is provided for your reference:

1. **List of worries**

   Example:

   - ☞ People I love are suffering from addiction and destroying their lives.

2. **Buckets**

NO CONTROL	PARTIAL CONTROL	TOTAL CONTROL
Example:		
What grown people choose to do to themselves and others.	*They are likely to be more motivated to get help if I stop enabling them. I can get out of their way.*	*I can put my energy into becoming a better person. I can resist judging or trying to fix other people.*

7
Investigate and Manage Fear

"There is a fine line between consciousness and obsession." — SAR

Fear has a powerful influence on what we think, how we feel, and what we do. It is triggered by the amygdala part of the brain, which is the defense mechanism that keeps us from harm and warns us about danger. Yet, if you are not aware of the power fear has over you, you can let threats of harm paralyze you from living a full life. I have learned that there is a fine line between consciousness and obsession. It is helpful to be aware of danger so you can avoid it. It is not helpful to allow your mind to conjure negative scenarios that inhibit your living freely.

In the movie *After Earth*, the character played by Will Smith tells his son, "Fear is imagined, danger is real." That message resonated with me because I am often consumed by dark imaginations of the worst-case scenario. I catch myself "awfulizing" and "future tripping" or "getting apocalyptic." When I do, I create unnecessary stress and block my own joy.

One of the most pervasive, mentally consuming fears I struggle with is related to harm coming to my children. Since they were babies, I've had deep anxieties about their health and safety. As a result, they experienced me as overprotective and controlling. I lost a lot of sleep and missed many joyful mothering moments.

I will never forget taking my youngest son, Sage, to overnight camp for the first time when he was about nine years old. My dad was visiting us from Minnesota and rode up with Scott and me to the camp, which was about two hours north of Atlanta. Sage was excited about going to stay-away camp, but I was terrified. The sick, sadistic story about how Jerry Sandusky, Penn State's assistant football coach, was sexually abusing young boys was unfolding repeatedly on the news. Just as my dad was reassuring me that everything would be fine, the digital sign hanging over the highway flashed in front of us. It read: "AMBER ALERT: CHILD ABDUCTION. WHITE SUV." It had the car's tag number and the number to call with information. That really set me off!

My fear transferred to Sage, who went from being excited to being anxious because I generated and transmitted that energy. For the entire week, I had insomnia, couldn't focus on my work, and ruminated (really obsessed) about Sage's well-being. I was upset because he didn't send a letter until day three! Meanwhile, he was having the time of his life and especially enjoying being out from underneath my propellers.

If I had anticipated the "best-case" scenario rather than always the "worst-case," I would have appreciated the present and experienced those moments fully. In hindsight, my fear and worry were a waste of time and energy. Sure, there are dangers in the world that could have brought my children harm. But I let fear distract me from the richness of the experience of watching them grow up. I learned that it is important to be aware of the degree to which negative thoughts and fears inhibit healthy child development and parent/child relationships.

Here are three lessons I have learned about investigating and managing fear:

LESSON #4

Identify the source of your fear

To address your fears, you must acknowledge, examine, and reconcile them. Journaling can be a great tool for getting out of your head. When you put your thoughts on paper, you can see them more clearly. When you find yourself caught up in fear, try writing your thought processes out:

- ☞ What are you afraid of?

- ☞ Where does it come from?

- ☞ Does it originate from stories or experiences with your kinfolk?

- ☞ Does it come from a past trauma you haven't processed yet?

- ☞ Is it based on a real, imminent risk, or is it just a scary story you are telling yourself?

- ☞ If it is based on real danger, how can you reduce the likely impact on you?

- ☞ If it is a fictitious scary story, how will you rewrite a more accurate narrative in your own head?

In *The Body Keeps the Score*, Dr. Bessel van der Kolk describes the perpetual state of fear that people who have a history of trauma experience

The elementary self-system in the brain stem and limbic system is massively activated when people are faced with the threat of annihilation, which results in an overwhelming sense of fear

and terror accompanied by intense physiological arousal. To people who are reliving a trauma, nothing makes sense; they are trapped in a life-or-death situation, a state of paralyzing fear or blind rage. Mind and body are constantly aroused, as if they are in imminent danger (Van der Kolk, 2014, p. 111).

When Scott and I started dating back in 1996, I was still hyper-vigilant about the possibility that he could be an abuser, a liar, or an all-out fraud. I didn't trust him, not because of anything he did, but rather the memories I was carrying around from past relationships. Once we were having a heated discussion (not even an argument) and standing across the room from each other. As he stepped forward to embrace me, my instincts told me to defend myself. I grabbed a canister of sugar and flung it at him, just missing his head as he ducked.

"I am not that guy!" he assured me. It took a long time to retrain my brain to accept that he was indeed trustworthy and would never lay a hand on me in any harmful way. Once I recognized that my fear was based on experiences with someone who was nothing like Scott, I let down my guard so I could receive his love fully.

LESSON #5

Calm the fear center of your brain

Since the amygdala is triggered by threats and dangers, you can pay attention to when it is overreacting to a stimulus. They call this the amygdala hijack because it can cause your imagination and threat response to take off out of control. Your threat-danger response is your protective instinct. It is very important because it ignites you into action when danger is real. However, when it gets hijacked, you can calm it down through a variety of techniques.

My friend Mitsuko Ito is an empowerment coach, a Tapping Circle facilitator, and a regular workshop presenter on stress management. She teaches a technique called Emotional Freedom Technique (EFT) Tapping www.mitsukoito.com (Ito, n.d.). This practice originated in Eastern medicine and is based on the polyvagal theory, which asserts that our bodies are strongly connected to the activities of the brain, particularly the amygdala, through the vagus nerves.

In EFT tapping, you gently tap on points on your body where the vagus nerves connect with the amygdala (Evidence Based EFT, 2024). These places include the crown of your head, above your eyebrows, under your eyes, between your nose and upper lip, your chest, rib cage, and the exterior side of your hand just under your pinky finger. It is an easy practice that you can do anywhere. I have even found it helpful in managing my low back pain, which is often triggered by stress.

One of my students, who was preparing to graduate at the end of the semester, described the most beneficial strategies they gained to calm themselves when they are stressed:

> *The different stress reduction mechanisms like mindfulness meditation or EFT tapping, both of which I never really practiced prior to this class, could be tools for me to help me manage this transition into this new environment.*

Another way to calm your fears is through deep breathing. It is like giving yourself CPR. Dr. Beth Cabrera, author of *Beyond Happy: Women, Work, and Well-being* (Cabrera, 2015), is an expert in the field of well-being and positive psychology. She was generous with her wisdom as a guest speaker for my class several times. She shared numerous cognitive and behavioral strategies for well-being, including how to do four-count breathing by inhaling deeply for four counts, holding for four counts, exhaling slowly for four counts, holding for four counts, then repeating three to five times. She also provided important insights into the relationship between our guts and our minds. She revealed many hidden secrets about ultra-processed foods. The better we eat, the better we think and feel.

Guided meditation is another technique for calming the fear response when you find your mind overreacting to a perceived threat. There are many good meditations accessible online. One of my favorite meditation leaders is Tara Brach (www.tarabrach.com), whom I discovered during COVID by using the Calm App. Meditation can help you release yourself from anxiety and worry by noticing what is happening in your mind and bringing your attention to the present.

When I was a young adult struggling with low self-esteem, self-destructive behaviors, and a trauma-stress response to almost everything, I found my way to the practice of Nichiren Buddhism. Part of this practice is to chant the words *Nam-myoho-renge-kyo* in front of a scroll containing Chinese and Sanskrit characters called a gohonzon. I engaged in this practice twice daily for more than ten years. More than the words I was chanting, the discipline of twice-daily meditation provided a consistent practice of reflection, meditation, and "a pledge to oneself to never yield to difficulties and to win over one's suffering" (SGI International, 2025). Chanting calmed the fear center of my brain, as it requires a breathing pattern that is steady and measured while creating a calming vibration in the environment.

LESSON #6

Generate hopeful and optimistic thoughts

Even though much of our thinking happens unconsciously, our minds are trainable. When you notice that your fear keeps you from experiencing real joy and is not based on the imminent threat of real danger, you can engage in a discussion with yourself (in writing, in your mind, or even aloud).

Here are some prompts to help you condition your mind to generate hopeful and optimistic thoughts rather than catastrophizing. When facing an adverse situation, consider:

- What do you **hope** will be the outcome in this situation?

- What is the **best** thing that could possibly happen?

- How can you **steer** this to a positive outcome?

- What **joy** could you experience if you release yourself from the grip of your fears?

Researchers have studied the relationship between hope for the future and our ability to thrive through difficulty. In one of the many studies proving this positive correlation, a scientific examination showed that people who intentionally engage in hopeful thoughts were able to reduce negative feelings when faced with adversity. They further proved that people who are generally more hopeful are less stressed by challenges and can recover from obstacles more quickly (Ong, Edwards, & Bergeman, 2006).

As a strategy consultant, I often use appreciative inquiry to galvanize people in organizations toward a positive future. The approach, developed by David Cooperrider at Case Western Reserve University, focuses on an organization's positive strengths (Cooperrider & Whitney, 2005). Rather than asking employees, "What is broken and needs to be fixed?" the questions are more related to "What are the strengths we can build on as we envision a better future?" We can draw out similar kinds of information in both lines of questioning. However, participants' energy is more optimistic and enthusiastic when we center the discussion around a strengths-based inquiry.

Appreciative inquiry can be a powerful tool for building organizational resilience as it "approaches resilience from the place of assisting leaders in developing their own understanding and personal call to resilience by using appreciative inquiry principles and practices" (McArthur-Blair & Cockell, 2018, p. 7).

Self-Reflection Activity:
INVESTIGATE AND MANAGE FEAR

We all have fears. Either we manage them, or they manage us. The first step is to define what they are, understand how they show up, explore where they come from, and identify some solutions to manage them.

In this activity, you will take four steps:

Step 1: List your fears. List the fears that have an impact on the quality of your life. Naming them can make them less scary.

Step 2: Identify the signs and symptoms. Describe the impact these fears have on you. What are the signs and symptoms that show how fear impacts your life?

Step 3: Discover the origins. Explore where the fears come from. Are they based on an actual present threat? Are they based on past harm you have experienced? Are they rooted in projections of a negative future?

Step 4: Find solutions. Plan to address the source of each fear and redirect your thoughts. If it is based on real danger, how can you reduce the risk of that danger? If it is not based on a real threat, how will you stop telling yourself scary stories, or "awfulizing"? If it is related to a past trauma you have endured, how will you resolve that history?

An example is provided first for your reference.

What is my fear?	How does this fear impact me?	Where does this fear come from?	What can I do about the impact of this fear?
Example: *Being involved in a car accident*	*Anxiety causes tension that makes me less nimble as I drive.* *My heart is racing, and breathing is shallow.* *I ride the brakes and avoid freeways*	*My wandering mind has caused past accidents.* *Knowledge that others drive distracted and impaired.* *Fear of injury and death.*	*Keep my attention focused on the present moment.* *Breathe to calm anxiety.* *Budget time to take the safest route.*

8

Reprogram Unhealthy Conditioning

"I've got a mean girl in my head, and she's only mean to one person." — SAR

We can be our own worst critics—even self-sabotaging bullies. There are many reasons for this, including social conditioning, early experiences, comparing ourselves with others, media influences, and a myriad of negative forces. The consequence of defeatist thinking is that it erodes our confidence or motivation to push through difficulty and limits our discovery of what we need to learn from adversity.

When I was reorganized out of my leadership role, I learned a powerful lesson about the importance of self-talk. My role had been divided up into four new roles and was now led by someone who had previously called herself my friend. Grasping for some certainty and a predictable employment future, I applied for every position they created. Each time, I was rejected. The new leader claimed I wasn't qualified for any of the roles and implied that I brought little value to the organization. At first, I rebuffed that assertion. But after months had passed, I began to internalize these messages.

Maybe I am not smart enough. Maybe I lack savvy and diplomacy to succeed as a leader, I thought. I really struggled through this period but was fortunate that I had decided to pursue my doctoral studies at that time. It just so happened that my first area of study was human development and the formation of self-esteem.

One of the most influential scholars in my early studies about self-perception and self-esteem was author bell hooks. Her book *Rock my soul: Black people and self-esteem* (hooks, 2003) gave me new insights into my own conditioning. In this unfiltered exploration of how societal racism and sexism warp our self-perception, hooks's work helped me understand how my negative thoughts and behaviors were shaped by a world that did not understand or accept my biracial identity.

In my adolescence and early adulthood, I thought of myself as "The Ugly Duckling," a reference to the story of a swan who was raised in a brood of ducks and made to feel inferior because he was different until he realized he was a beautiful and elegant swan (Anderson, 1965). As I got older, I adopted the **swan** as my identity symbol and took it as my nickname to acknowledge that I had freed myself from an inferiority complex. The "otherness" I'd experienced in being different from my kinfolk and classmates had me feeling like I was "less than" until I learned that I had been taught so many lies about what constitutes beauty.

A self-defeating mindset can lead you to settle for less than you deserve, compromise your values, or jettison your goals.

When I began teaching resilience to college students, I discovered the powerful work of psychologist and author Kristin Neff, an expert on self-compassion. Neff describes self-compassion as "being supportive toward oneself when experiencing suffering or pain—be it caused by personal mistakes and inadequacies or external life challenges" (Neff, 2023, p. 193). She developed a theoretical model that can be helpful when you find yourself caught up in self-harming thoughts and behaviors. The elements of her model include understanding these internal conversations and addressing them as you recognize what is helpful and what is harmful.

The model describes helpful elements:

Self-kindness:
I try to be loving towards myself when I'm feeling emotional pain.

Common humanity:
When things are going badly for me, I see the difficulties as part of life that everyone goes through.

Mindfulness:
When I'm feeling down, I try to approach my feelings with curiosity and openness.

And harmful elements:

Self-judgment:
I'm disapproving and judgmental about my own flaws and inadequacies.

Isolation:
When I think about my inadequacies it tends to make me feel more separate and cut off from the rest of the world.

Overidentification:
When something upsets me, I get carried away with my feelings.
(Neff, 2023, p. 197).

Since discovering Neff's work, I have applied much of what I learned about self-compassion from her and Tara Brach, who teaches a concept called radical acceptance (Brach, 2004). These tools have given me a way out of self-defeating negative thinking, especially when I find myself amid crisis, challenge, or change.

Here are three lessons I learned to reprogram my unhealthy thinking and behaviors:

LESSON #7

Pay attention to your inner voice

You can't change a narrative you do not know is present. I often say, "I have a mean girl in my head, and she is only mean to one person—me." So many of our internal conversations take place deep within the subconscious. Like a computer's operating system, it works in the background to insidiously influence thoughts and actions. Early experiences with kinfolk are a major source of influence on this programming.

I have learned how to hush my inner voice when it repeats the bullying taunts from my middle school classmates.

"Monkey face!" they used to call me. They named me Taco to degrade my Latina identity. I gently tell myself, "That's not you. They did not know you, and they did not appreciate you." When the little girl in my head replays the words from my adoptive grandmother—"You're not as smart or as pretty as your sister"—I must put that voice in check.

Stay attentive to the subtle, yet influential, self-talk that results from negative conditioning. Understand where it comes from, whether it be childhood influences or adulthood experiences. Notice the lies you have been told about yourself and how you might be repeating them to yourself. Did someone tell you that you should not be good at something because of who you are? Were you led to believe that you were not as good as someone else for one reason or another? Have you been tricked into accepting that you are less worthy than others? How have the media and broader society shaped your self-perception?

In my doctoral studies about human development and social psychology, I learned from the work of pioneering social psychologist Gordon Allport that the human psyche does two things instinctively. First, it works to protect our self-esteem. Second, it works to minimize our discomfort (Allport, 1954).

When a person feels inferior to another, they might put that other person down so they can preserve a favorable perception of themselves.

I heard this play out when my maternal grandmother said, "We may be poor white trash, but at least we aren't [n-word]." If a person feels uncomfortable when another challenges their assumptions or thinking, their psyche might compel them to push the other person away. When I was a small child, I heard my adoptive grandparents whispering about avoiding certain neighborhoods because they were "too colorful." Learning about these psychological processes in my studies gave me such relief. I learned that their harmful words of criticism and condemnation toward me were not because I was a bad person, but rather their own prejudicial conditioning.

LESSON #8

Focus on your strengths

Positive self-talk can feel unnatural, so it takes practice. Part of my social conditioning has taught me that practicing humility and modesty is the best way to avoid conflict and negative attention from others. I usually don't talk about my strengths and capabilities out loud, nor do I talk about them through my inner voice.

In her world-renowned book *Mindset*, psychologist Carol Dweck demonstrates the relationship between how we think about our capabilities and our ultimate success in every facet of life (professional, academic, competitive sports, etc.) (Dweck, 2016). She argues that there are two mindsets that shape how we see the world and our place in it. A fixed mindset is a belief that our capabilities, attributes, and success in life are predetermined and unlikely to be altered. A growth mindset is the belief that our success can be cultivated through continuous development and effort. She shows evidence that these mindsets "change what people strive for and what they see as success. How they change the definition, significance, and impact of failure. And how they change the deepest meaning of effort" (Dweck, 2016, p. 11).

For many years, I engaged in self-loathing, self-pity, and self-harm. I had internalized many of the negative messages I received from ignorant and hurtful people during my adolescence. I ruminated about my failures and felt shame about my mistakes. When I began to practice daily journaling with positive discussion prompts, my narrative about myself began to shift. I started with simple journal prompts:

What did I do well today?

What am I proud of today?

What did I learn today?

After practicing this consistently for about three years, my mindset began to shift. I was able to look ahead and declare a vision for the life I wanted—and consistency was key. I created a reality for my life that was greater than I would have ever believed when I was looking at myself through my deficiencies.

Many people have been programmed to see their limits and challenges before possibilities and opportunities. If this is your reality, you must stretch here to quiet those pessimistic voices and release yourself from the bondage of thinking small.

LESSON #9

Savor the good

Have you ever eaten something that tastes so good, you didn't want to swallow it? Have you ever had an experience so elating that you didn't want it to ever end? Throughout our busy daily lives, we usually breeze from one thing to the next, paying little attention to the tastes, sounds, smells, or feelings that bring us joy.

Savoring is the practice of intentionally holding your attention to the positive things you encounter—whether it be a soft melody that relaxes you, a sweet smell that crosses your nose, a kind interaction with another person, or a proud moment when you succeed at something you worked for. The practice of savoring involves simple acts, such as pausing to admire the beauty of your surroundings or putting your phone away so you can engage fully in a conversation with someone you value and respect.

Whenever I get in my kayak for a few hours on the lake, I am intentional about being fully present in that experience. As a person with a compulsively wandering mind, it does require repetitive redirection. I usually start out well by drinking in the beautiful scenery as the sky and glistening water dance with each other in front of my boat. I love feeling the waves from the speedboats raise and drop my kayak like an amusement park ride. But invariably, by the time I get a good stride of strokes with my paddle, my mind goes back to something I did that I wish I hadn't done, or it ventures forward to a worry about the future.

I often say out loud, "Sonia, stay present. This is time that you have earned to enjoy a calm space in nature." Then I just keep paddling. I can beckon this experience later when I am in the throes of a crisis. Drawing this beautiful moment forward will remind me that experiences are momentary.

There is empirical evidence that savoring has direct relationships to resilience and a positive quality of life. In *Savoring: A New Model of Positive Experience*, Bryant and Veroff explain the benefits of savoring that go well beyond navigating adversity:

Being able to handle adversity is vital in life, but having a capacity to cope seems not to be the same as having the capacity to enjoy life. In other words, just because people are not down, doesn't mean they're up ... We contend that savoring is this missing process—the positive counterpart of coping (Bryant & Veroff, 2017, p. 1 & 2).

They also contend that engaging in an "active process of enjoyment" (p. 3) prepares us for adversity, challenge, and change by training our minds and attention to gravitate toward things that can give us strength and hope. It is a life practice that requires being attentive to our blessings and the present moments that enrich us.

Savoring is not only vital for your readiness to deal with difficulty, but it is an essential part of responding to and recovering from adverse events. Research has shown that there is a "coping–savoring link forming upward spirals implicated in individuals' overall well-being" (Tao, et al., Feb 2024, p. 172), meaning that habits of savoring help us not only get through the difficulties while they are happening, but they have more long-term, enduring, positive effects in the aftermath.

Self-Reflection Activity:
MINDFUL SELF-COMPASSION

I developed the following model based on a range of research and literature about mindfulness and self-compassion, largely influenced by the work of Neff (2023) and Allport (1954). It situates a range of possible reactions to adversity along a continuum of thoughts and actions ranging from compassionate to abusive.

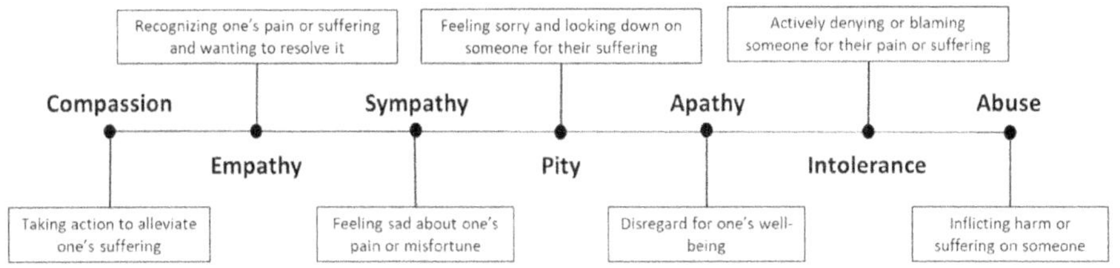

Figure 8. Compassion Continuum

Review the model from left to right, then consider the following:

- ☞ What might a person say or do if they are compassionate, empathetic, sympathetic, pitiful, apathetic, intolerant, or abusive?

- ☞ How might those words and actions play out if they are directed inwardly at oneself?

Then, follow these three steps to complete the activity:

Step 1: Reflect on a situation (past, current, or anticipated future) where someone you love experiences adversity, challenge, or change. What did/would you say to them? What did/would you do for them?

Step 2: Reflect on a situation where you (past, current, or anticipated future) experience adversity, challenge, or change. What did/should your inner voice say? What did/should you do for yourself?

Step 3: What do you notice about the way you respond to those you care about and the way you respond to yourself? Are there opportunities for you to show yourself more compassion in the future? If so, how will you do that?

An example is provided first for your reference on the following page.

Example:

A Loved One's Adversity

My friend was fired from his job after being accused of accessing unauthorized files. He was adamant he did not access the files, but his employer did not believe him.

What did you say?	I told him I believed in him and that I would stand by him. I listened without judging him.
What did you do?	I helped him get his resume together and introduced him to people who had connections.
What type of response was it?	I showed him compassion. I worked to help relieve him of his suffering.

Your Own Adversity

I was impacted by an organizational restructuring and was moved out of my position without an explanation.

What did you say?	I told myself I must not be good enough and that people did not have confidence in me, respect me, or value my work.
What did you do?	I ruminated repeatedly about what I should have and could have done better.
What type of response was it?	I reacted with self-pity and self-apathy. I internalized self-critical ideas.

How will you show yourself compassion in the future?

- ~ I will recognize that people make decisions that impact me for reasons I do not fully understand or agree with.

- ~ I will focus on what I can control. I will give my best. And if that is not enough, I will find an alternative situation.

Now, it's your turn:

A Loved One's Adversity

What did you say?	
What did you do?	
What type of response was it?	

Your Own Adversity

What did you say?	
What did you do?	
What type of response was it?	

How will you show yourself compassion in the future?

9

Seek Healthy Support

"Learn from the mistakes of others. You'll never live long enough to make them all yourself." —Author Unknown

The need for human connection is amplified anytime we encounter a challenge or a change. Even when change is positive and planned, having someone to enjoy it with makes it even more rewarding.

When I was a young, single mother, the relationships most central to my life were with my children and my mother. They were a powerful source of strength and inspiration for me. At the same time, I learned that I needed relationships with others outside my nuclear family to help me navigate challenges and celebrate successes. I needed people who related to my experience.

Playdates and birthday parties became my main social interactions. These acquaintances became my tribe and provided an important source of social support for me as a struggling, single mom. I felt like I belonged with them. Even though I worked and went to college for eighteen years (earning four degrees at a steady pace), I still made time for these relationships as an outlet from the day-to-day demands.

After I married, I kept in touch with my friends, even though we didn't get together as frequently. My husband became my primary source of emotional support, but there were times when I needed someone more neutral and objective to talk things through with.

My closest friends have been my strength in getting through the hardest times of life, and they have joined me in celebrating my proudest moments. When Scott was sick in the hospital, and then after he died, my friends were the glue that held me together emotionally. They sat with me at the hospital, hung out with my boys after school, took me to the gym to work off my anxiety, went with me to the movies, and did so many other things that helped me deal with the tremendous loss.

The most important relationship as I healed and navigated my newfound status as a widow was with another widow. My dear friend Charlotte lost her husband just five years earlier, when she was also forty-four years old (same age I was when Scott died). I think of her as a Sherpa, the highly skilled people who help travelers navigate the rugged and difficult terrain of the Himalaya Mountains. She knew that difficult road and understood my pain, fear, uncertainty, and grief. She showed me that joy was possible again. She helped me decide when and how I would venture out into the dating world again. She encouraged me to keep swiping left, bypassing anyone who would not be a positive addition to my life. She supported me while I learned to live by myself and with myself, and to truly love myself.

After five years as a widow, I met a kind, generous, and loving man named Wesley who treated me like a queen. When he proposed to me after four years of dating, Charlotte was ecstatic. "Just go ahead and marry that man!" she said. And I did. It was a great decision, and I was able to make it with confidence by talking it through with someone who had walked the same path.

Navigating change, whether personal or professional, often involves confusion, chaos, fear, and pain. Competent and neutral therapists, counselors, and coaches have helped me consider my options so I could make the best decisions for my life based on where I was and where I wanted to go.

Even as a change practitioner myself, I have come to rely on objective insight offered by counselors and mentors to help me deal with changes. Finding the right counselor was a bit of a challenge. In my early days as a widow, I had a session with a therapist who told me to "Just go do some retail therapy to take your mind off of it."

Shopping? WTF? That was not helpful guidance, especially as I was once again leading a single-income family. I had to be persistent and keep looking for a therapist who would bring valuable insights. Eventually, I did, and it was helpful.

Today, I get extraordinary support from a community of people I know only through weekly Zoom support group meetings. In this community, we don't need to know each other to support each other. In fact, anonymity is an expectation in the group. It is a support group for those who love people suffering from the disease of addiction. In the nightly meetings, members share experiences, strength, and hope so that no one has to go through this reality alone. We don't question, judge, or give advice to each other. We share only our own perspectives and insights so that others may also benefit from what we are learning on our journey (www.nar-anon.org). I choose what to pick up from what others are putting down.

I started going to these meetings because I was looking for specific strategies to cure my loved one. I wanted the silver bullet to fix this problem. In one of the first meetings I attended, I learned about The Three C's: I didn't **cause** it, I can't **cure** it, and I can't **control** it. They helped me see that the only thing I can control is the work I do to better myself. They taught me how to love without enabling and detach myself from other people's problems, even when I love them deeply. This group has been a lifeline for me during this very difficult time.

Here are three lessons I have learned about seeking healthy support.

LESSON #10

Talk to those who have "seen the movie"

When you are going through something challenging (especially for the first time), it can help you to understand how other people have handled the same or similar situations. Find resources that offer perspectives and insights to help you prepare for, respond to, and recover from challenges.

Workplace resources, such as employee assistance programs and employee resource groups, can provide support for managing change and adversity in both personal and professional contexts. Having close friends at work has been extremely important for my emotional and social well-being.

Working for a Big Four global consulting firm taught me how to combat imposter syndrome. Like the culture of an elite college, imposter syndrome is a pervasive mindset in a preeminent brand. Highly talented people who have extraordinary credentials and work hard still doubt whether they are worthy of being there. I was one of those people until I took the initiative to find mentors who helped me look at the situation in context. They gave me guidance to understand the dynamics of serving clients and keeping leaders happy while adding measurable value. To accept their insight, I had to put down my guard and be open to honest feedback.

Social media, despite its negative effects, can also be helpful in finding others who share your experiences. After his kidney transplant in 2020, Wesley found a Facebook group of others who shared that experience. It has been very helpful for him in understanding common experiences. Members of this group share insights into the side effects of the new organ and medications to keep it viable.

Many churches offer support groups that are open to people outside the congregation and include topics such as unemployment, grief and loss, addiction, financial issues, and more. These resources let people know that they are not alone.

Community service organizations, such as the Alzheimer's Association, the Association for Suicide Prevention, Alcoholics Anonymous, Survivors of Suicide, Gambling Anonymous, National Alliance for Mental Illness, and many more, provide support groups and a plethora of online education and resources. By seeking reliable resources, you can gain information that will help you navigate difficult experiences through the lessons others have learned.

LESSON #11

Define your circles of trust

In *Daring Greatly*, scholar and author Brené Brown recommends, "Get a one-inch piece by one-inch piece of paper and write down the names of the people whose opinions matter to you. It needs to be small because it forces you to edit" (Brown, 2012, p. 22). Her rules for this short list are simple. It can contain only people who you know love and care about you, who do not have any ulterior motives, and who will be honest with you (even if they tell you things you don't want to hear). Her guidance is to give weight only to criticism that comes from this short list of people because they are the ones who really matter the most.

I challenged the students in my resilience class to do this exercise. One of them asked me, "What if I don't even have one person to list?" I encouraged him to make building relationships a priority and seek out like-minded people he could get to know and trust. At the end of the semester, he thanked me:

"Before this class, I would have never made it a priority to build relationships with others. All I was doing was going to class, studying, and playing video games online. But now through this class, I have made friendships with three people who I really like and feel I can trust.

I have a very small circle of friends I consider to be my most trusted confidants (my inner circle of trust), a next layer of friends who I value but don't share everything with, and a broader circle of acquaintances who are part of my community. They all have an important role in my life, but the roles are different.

The distinction hasn't always been clear to me. Over time, I learned how to categorize relationships so I can set healthy boundaries for myself and others. Defining these roles for the people in my life helps me manage my own expectations and set parameters for how to engage them.

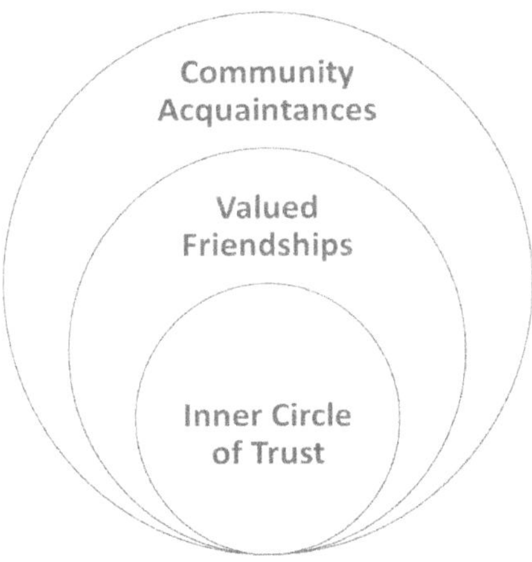

Figure 9. Circles of Trust

When I experience self-doubt or face a difficult decision, I go first to my inner circle of trust. When I face a work-related challenge and need guidance, I usually engage colleagues I also consider to be valued friends. When I celebrate more public achievements, I engage community acquaintances.

Early in my time at the university where I work now, I was invited to speak as part of an employee resource group panel. I shared my story about losing Scott and making a career change. Several people from the audience approached me afterward because they, too, experienced loss of a loved one or a major career change. Following that first conversation two colleagues, Pearl and Cheryl, invited me join with them in creating the first employee resource group focused on resilience. Later, they asked me to lead it. Unlike the affinity groups organized around gender or racial identity, our group created community for those navigating adversity, challenge, or change. It became a place where participants connected with community acquaintances, developed valued friendships, and sometimes even established an inner circle of trust.

LESSON #12

Nurture your spirituality

Healthy support can also come from a connection to spiritual energy, whether that be in the form of a Higher Power, God, Allah, or whatever source inspires you. Even if you don't believe that there is a power greater than yourself, you can find healing and comfort in connecting to spiritual energy. I am referring to an awareness of the fact that there are forces at play in the universe around us that are outside our control. I have learned to give myself healthy support by creating space for reflection, meditation, and prayer.

Every evening before I go to sleep, I spend ten minutes reflecting on the things I am thankful for and what I learned that day. It reminds me that my experiences are not all due to my own actions, but to a force of energy that is greater than mine.

It also reminds me that my lived experience is always shaped by how I react to the things outside my control.

Here is an example of one of my prayers: "My Creator, thank you for the blessing of this day. For not one more is guaranteed. Today, I learned the power of patience. I wanted something very badly, but it just was not coming to fruition. I tried to make it happen for myself, but you knew better for me. For at the time, I felt like I was being deprived of this thing I wanted so much. But today, I learned the truth. I was protected. It would have been an unhealthy situation that might have set me back. Thank you for your protection."

Some people find strength through a faith community. In connection with others who share their values and beliefs, they find comfort and direction. A faith community does not have to be tied to a church or religious doctrine. It can consist of a small group of close friends who share a belief in a Higher Power.

Group yoga has been proven to deliver powerful physical, emotional, and spiritual benefits to those who practice. In The Body Keeps the Score, van der Kolk describes how yoga has been used as trauma therapy with powerful positive results. "Actions that involve noticing and befriending the sensations in our bodies can produce profound changes in both mind and brain that can lead to healing from trauma" (p. 295). By nurturing your body, you can also nurture your spirit and mind.

In my early twenties, I was trapped in a spiral of self-destructive, reckless behavior. Day after day, I woke up with regret. My behavior reinforced my inner voice, which told me I was not worthy of love or success. Then I met Thembi, a petite Black woman with long salt-and-pepper braids. She was short in stature but enormous in strength and insight. She taught me about Buddhism and the laws of cause and effect. I learned that if I wanted to create a better life, I needed to envision and become a better person. Her gentle voice almost whispered to me, "If you want to change the shape of the shadow being cast by a tree, you must change the shape of the tree. Your life is but a reflection of your spirit right now. To change your circumstances is to change your heart first so that you can create better karma."

She taught me the discipline of chanting every morning and every night. The consistency of this practice helped my mind focus on what I could become instead of ruminating on my shame. The readings and teachings of Nichiren Daishonin gave me insight into how I could change my karma and live a better life. I believed it was working. Therefore, it did work. I stopped engaging in harmful behavior and started taking care of myself. I became a better person with a more positive self-perception. As a result, I became a better parent, employee, daughter, and friend.

When I started dating Scott, who was a devout Christian, he shared *Conversations with God,* in which the author describes the vital role of prayer and intentional connection with our Creator:

> *The difficulty is knowing the difference between messages from God and data from other sources. Discrimination is a simple matter with the application of a basic rule: Mine is always your Highest Thought, your Clearest Word, your Grandest feeling. Anything less is from another source ... The Highest Thought is always that thought which contains joy. The Clearest Words are those words which contain truth. The Grandest Feeling is that feeling which you call love. (Walsch, 1995)*

Self-Reflection Activity:
CREATING A BOARD OF DIRECTORS

Sometimes, we hesitate to reach out for help or support from others because we are ashamed, too proud, or don't want to be a burden to anyone. We might struggle or suffer through difficulties alone because we don't have a person we trust. Sometimes, we have a professional situation that people in our inner circle of trust can't understand. Or maybe we have a personal situation we don't want to share with our colleagues. A board of directors can advise us across a range of situations.

In this activity, you will take three steps:

Step 1: Consider the various contexts of your life where support will be important. What are those contexts?

Step 2: Identify one or two people you might rely on for healthy support in each context. The criteria for everyone include:

- ☞ You believe they have your best interests at heart.

- ☞ You believe they will be honest with you.

- ☞ They have knowledge and experience that is different from yours.

Step 3: Define how you will engage them.

An example is shown below for your reference:

Context	People With Helpful Insight	How I Can Engage Them
Example: Difficult situations I face as a mother.	☞ My mom ☞ My therapist	☞ Call her when I need ☞ Schedule a virtual coaching appointment

10

Take Time for Self-Care

"If I don't show care for myself, how can I expect anyone else to?" — SAR

During times of loss, uncertainty, change, and challenges with kinfolk, your energy can become depleted. You might put your own needs at the bottom of your priority list. Your physical, emotional, social, spiritual, and financial needs may take a back seat when you are intensely focused on solving a problem or fulfilling your responsibilities. You may feel resentful when you do things for others at your own expense. These dynamics can create toxic stress that makes your own healing difficult.

Creating an intentional time and place to regenerate and recover from stressors is critical for achieving clarity, strength, and fortitude. Refueling your tank is important for your overall well-being and vital if you want to effectively manage difficulties. As my friend Dr. Joi Alexander often tells my students, "self-care isn't selfish."

In *When the Body Says No: The Hidden Cost of Stress*, Gabor Maté provides evidence of the complex interdependent relationship between our bodies and minds. He describes psychoneuroimmunoendocrinology (PNIE), which is the study of interactions among the mind, the nervous system, and health. This interdisciplinary body of knowledge examines the complex interplay between experiences and well-being, reaffirming the importance of taking time to care for ourselves in all three realms: mental well-being, physical well-being, and social/emotional well-being.

When I was a young, single mom and my older boys were early-elementary age, I worked full-time and took classes at the Minneapolis Community and Technical College. I would leave early in the mornings to drop them off at before-school day care, work all day, pick them up from after-school day care, go home and cook dinner, help them with homework, do bathtime, read bedtime stories, then spend the next several hours doing my own schoolwork. I did this for seven years until I finally earned my undergraduate degree from Metropolitan State University. I pushed through the days with an average of five hours of sleep.

As I look back on those seven years, I know I was often run down, sleep-deprived, and emotionally exhausted. I did not understand or appreciate the value of self-care. As a result, I did not always make the best decisions for myself or my children. I was vulnerable to being manipulated by others and did not think as clearly as I needed to. I can attribute many regrettable moments to poor decision-making that was largely the result of failure to care for myself.

I married Scott six months after I graduated with my bachelor's degree. Then I spent four more years working on my first master's degree, then another seven years earning my PhD while managing a stressful full-time career and raising three sons.

Although I had a husband, I still wasn't taking very good care of myself. I did my best to give attention and guidance to my sons. Two were entering their teens, and the youngest was born while I was in graduate school. I spent my free time doing freelance writing for local newspapers and national magazines or investing in real estate. I was always on the move and filled every day from end to end with busyness.

Resilience expert Linda Hoopes is the author of *Prosilience: Building Your Resilience for a Turbulent World*, which offers helpful insights for personal and organizational resilience (Hoopes, 2017). Her research and practice have shown the importance of managing energy when facing challenges. First, she teaches that challenges are not inherently bad but rather provide opportunities for growth and development. She teaches strategies for protecting, building, and replenishing mental, emotional, and physical energy, all of which are essential for healing and restoration.

Self-care does not require an expensive or long vacation. You can generate energy through daily practices. But first, you may need to reprogram yourself when it comes to self-care.

I have been programmed to think I do not deserve to rest, relax, refresh, and renew. For me, taking time for self-care has been one of the most challenging parts of building resilience. I have been conditioned to believe that my value is in my actions (what I do) and my achievements (what I have). I have put extraordinary effort into both of these.

Now that I am gaining lessons in resilience, I am reprogramming my life to turn toward who I am and how I treat myself (self-care). It has required an intellectual shift, but also a complete change in my beliefs about myself and the actions I take toward myself. To reframe my mindset, I repeatedly tell myself:

- ☞ I must be as important to myself as everyone else is to me.

- ☞ I have a right to enjoy peace and quiet.

- ☞ I can make space and time for myself and still maintain important relationships.

- ☞ When I give my best, I have given enough.

- ☞ I must be as kind to myself as I am to my best friend.

As one of my students so eloquently described in their resilience plan paper,

> *After learning the importance of self-care time, I found that I had not been prioritizing myself the way that a more resilient person should. Mainly, I have identified that I struggle to maintain a schedule, and properly manage time, so I hardly ever allot time for myself. Throughout the day, I find myself simply saying yes to things that I have no time for. Additionally, I will get to the end of the day immensely frustrated at the things that I didn't get done that I had intended to accomplish. This class inspired me to start prioritizing my time and my daily needs, so that I can start to take more control of my own time.*

From what I have learned through life and teaching, I want to share three main lessons about taking time for self-care.

LESSON #13

Set healthy boundaries

Boundaries are an expression of love, for us and others, as they keep relationships in balance. In the face of adversity, you need energy and resources to make good decisions and navigate difficulties. Boundaries allow you to manage your time, energy, and resources so you can effectively respond and recover from challenges.

Being aware of codependent relationships is an important part of establishing boundaries. Codependency is an unhealthy attachment to any person or relationship that is "one-sided, emotionally destructive, and/or abusive" (Mental Health America, 2024). I have never known a person who intended to get caught up in a codependent relationship, yet many (including myself) have found themselves in one. I can admit without shame that I let dysfunctional relationships go on for far too long—with kinfolk, platonic friends, romantic partners, work colleagues, and even neighbors.

While it is always best to set boundaries in the beginning of any relationship, it is possible to create them after a relationship has been established. Even with our kinfolk, we can reset boundaries at any time. Setting healthy boundaries requires honest and compassionate dialogue. "Honesty without compassion is brutal. Compassion without honesty is enabling" (Willock, 2024). Speaking up for yourself can be unfamiliar and even uncomfortable. But when it is safe to do so, a one-sided and depleting relationship can become mutually beneficial and rewarding.

It can be hard to tell someone when you need to draw the line, particularly if they lack compassion and care for your well-being. Sometimes, it can be dangerous, so you must take caution in how you do it. When setting a boundary with an emotionally unstable person, it is best to enlist the help of others to bolster your protection.

I have learned so much about the importance of boundaries by participating in the Nar-Anon twelve-step program. I have learned how to respect the boundaries of my addicted loved one, even though my instinct is to rescue, intervene, and intrude in their life. Watching helplessly as someone I love throws their life away has been agonizing. But the program has taught me that I can't control or cure them. I can, however, show love and assist them in getting help when they are ready to change.

I have learned that trying to rescue them or inappropriately assuming their responsibilities impedes them from finding the motivation to change.

"Hands off pays off," explained Karen Willock, therapist at Treehouse Recovery, in her YouTube video titled *How to Say No to an Addict* (Willock, 2024). We enable others when we solve problems that are not ours to fix. I am learning to apply this approach with many people in my life. They have a Savior, and it's not me.

Boundaries are important not only when it comes to relationships with people. They are also important for responsibilities. One of the last text messages Scott sent was to his friend Henry, whom he told, "Man, I can't wait to see you at Sonia's graduation. She will finally be done with school. I will finally get my wife back!" I learned about this message after he passed away. It hurt me to know how much Scott longed for my time and attention when I was so consumed with my ambitions. I'd failed to set healthy work and school boundaries. As a result, I missed out on the gift of that time with him.

I can't change anything about the past, but I can use it to inform my present and future. Today, I am married to a man who lovingly nudges me when I am consumed by work and out of balance. Wesley has no problem reminding me that not one more day is guaranteed and that the only thing we know for sure is this moment right now. My life can slide out of balance without my even realizing it. Having an accountability partner helps bring it back into balance. I also need to self-regulate. To be at the top of my game, my physical, emotional, and spiritual battery needs to be charged enough to power me through the challenging times. I wish I'd understood this earlier in my life, but I am now finally breaking free from my addiction to the grind.

LESSON #14

Prioritize rest

In her powerful work *Rest Is Resistance*, author Tricia Hersey (2022) describes how we can become brainwashed by the "grind culture" that fools us into believing that success is all about money, consumption, and material wealth, even at our own peril. She asserts that our capitalistic society has us believing that our worth is associated with how much we produce and that our system is designed to exploit and dehumanize us. Rest, she argues, is the purest form of human need and is essential to our personal power.

She says, "We are not resting to be productive. We are resting simply because it is our divine right to do so." (p. 62). She writes about how her grandmother would close her eyes while sitting up for thirty minutes every day to reclaim a moment of her own humanity and sanity.

Rest can be very difficult for ambitious, industrious, and determined people who want to succeed. I recall vividly when my youngest son, Sage, was nine months old and Scott was in the hospital, fighting for his life through a terrible sickle cell crisis. It was touch and go for more than a week. The doctors didn't know if he was going to survive, and I was trying to keep round-the-clock watch over him at the hospital. I was nursing my baby, so I'd pack him up and take him to and from the hospital with me. I was exhausted. One day, I went home in the middle of the afternoon to care for my two teenage boys and clean up the house. I lay down on the bed for what I thought would be just a moment. I woke up more than an hour later, just as Sage was rolling toward the edge of the bed. I grabbed him by the ankle just in time to prevent him from falling headfirst onto the hardwood floors. Sleep deprivation had taken over.

In times of major crisis, you may not have the luxury to prioritize rest. That is why it is important to establish a habit of sleeping on a regular schedule, free from distractions. When you build the practice of rest during the calm times, you will be more inclined to find ways to rest during times of calamity.

Even during a busy or stressful workday, I am learning to prioritize the strategic pause that my mind, eyes, mouth, and body need. Sometimes, I resist resting because I have not completed all my assigned tasks for the day. But I remind myself that if I do not rest by choice, my body will rebel and make me do so.

LESSON #15

Stack healthy habits

Healthy habits build nimbleness, strength, and stability in every realm of your life. If you start with a deficit, such as being born into intergenerational poverty or a cycle of family violence, this can be difficult, but it is possible. My mother taught me how to invest in real estate, harness creativity through art, exercise while doing housework, and pray for guidance. She learned none of these things from her abusive, alcohol-dependent parents. She broke the intergenerational cycle of destructive, self-harming behaviors through her determination to have (and give me) a better life.

I have found that resilience is built through habits in five areas that can be stacked on top of each other for maximum impact:

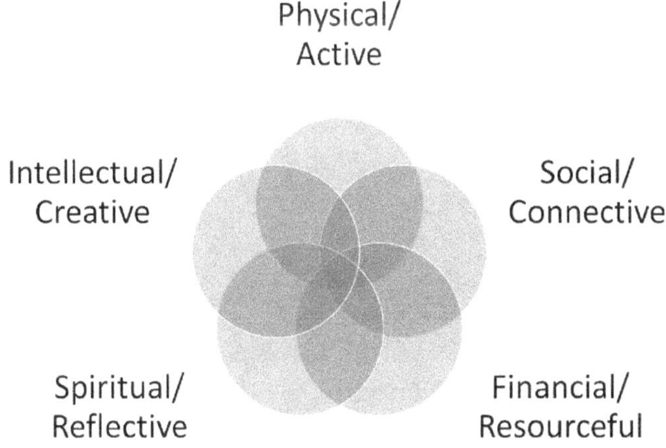

Figure 10. Resilience Habits

Physical/active habits include being intentional about what you eat, drink, do, or don't do. I am learning that the best way to build healthy physical habits is to take one step at a time. If I walk around the block once today, I will do it twice tomorrow. Abstaining from alcohol and avoiding sugary or ultra-processed foods can be a challenge. I know that I must be gentle with myself and keep trying, even when I struggle, so I can have a more active life.

When my older boys were small and we lived in public housing, I exercised by having them sit on my feet while I did sit-ups. They thought it was hilarious, but it helped me build my core. I used bags of sugar for weights as I built my arm muscles. Squats are one of the most important exercises for people over fifty as they prepare your core to get you off a chair, bed, or toilet. All these activities are free, but they do require discipline to make them a routine.

Intellectual/creative habits include exercising your mind and generating creativity by reading, learning, and thinking. One of my students highlighted one way they will build healthier intellectual habits:

> *Social media can also be very fake at times and spending a lot of time catching up with everyone's lives as opposed to focusing on yourself can leave you feeling empty at the end of the day. Most of us have developed a certain level of cell phone dependency. I notice that I feel anxious when I do not have my phone and I believe that managing this could be a great opportunity.*

Spiritual, reflective habits include making meditation and prayer—without distraction from other sources—a priority. For me, daily journaling has been vital.

One of my students offered ideas for how they will build stronger spiritual and reflective habits: "Recognize things that give meaning to my life; set aside time for thought and reflection; and participate in a cause that is important to me."

Another shared:

> *I will continue to lean into my faith, especially when harder times come rather than shying away from it. I will embrace my spiritual roots knowing that it will sustain me. Another thing that will help is listening to music whether it's alternative, gospel, or other genres that speaks to who I am as a person and my soul, and that will remain a vital part of my self-care.*

Social, connective habits include connecting regularly with people who care about me and whom I feel safe with. Social fitness means that relationships are mutually beneficial, two-way exchanges of care and affection. I schedule time for fun with my circle of friends and set the expectation with my husband that sisterhood is part of my well-being practice.

One of my students included the following social self-care action they will take:

> *I've recognized a tendency to avoid relying on others, a trait that has occasionally led to feelings of loneliness. I acknowledge this as my primary shortcoming and I'm willing to address it by confronting my lizard brain, the primal instinct to remain within my comfort zone. This would be actively engaging with others, expanding my social circle, and fostering new connections.*

Financial and resourceful habits involve balancing earnings, spending, investing, and saving. When I was a single mom barely able to put food on the table, I struggled to put money aside for the future. However, my employer had a deferred compensation program that let me use $25 from each check to purchase savings bonds. It added up and grew with interest. It was one way to make money without having to labor for it. That amount was a big sacrifice at the time, but once I got used to it being taken out, I learned how to adjust my spending. Saving money isn't easy because I have been conditioned to be a consumer and spend what I earn (or even more than I earn).

In their resilience plan, one of my students shared:

> *For financial, something that I struggle with is finding the balance between spending my money on having fun and saving it for the future and between eating out and cooking. As I start earning more with my new job, I will make a budget for myself and set some of my paycheck out for fun activities and eating out so that I more responsibly have fun and eat out while also saving for the future.*

Building consistency and stacking habits can strengthen your readiness to respond and recover from loss, uncertainty, change, and dealing with your kinfolk. For example, I can make a healthy, cost-effective meal (physical and financial) to share with friends (social) over a discussion about resilience (intellectual).

Self-Reflection Activity:
FIVE DAYS OF SELF-CARE

A daily practice of self-care can begin with one simple action in just one day. Each following day, you can add more actions to build a practice that can lead to consistency—if you are intentional. Even if you don't do much for yourself today, you can gradually build a habit using twelve simple actions.

For five consecutive days, keep track of the actions you take in a twenty-four-hour period. The chart below lists twelve actions you can try. You can also add your own. For each day, mark one point with an X or check mark. Gradually increase your self-care practices one day at a time. Add up the number of actions on the row to see how you progress over the five days.

Be gentle with yourself if you don't get it perfect the first time. Just do as much as you can for the five days. Then you can start again as many times as you want. The nice thing is that if you are blessed to live another day, you can try again.

Five-Day Self-Care Habit Builder

Self-Care Action	Day 1	Day 2	Day 3	Day 4	Day 5
1. Drank 36 oz. of water					
2. Slept 8 straight hours					
3. Got 30 minutes of exercise					
4. Set a healthy boundary for yourself or others					
5. Talked to someone who cares about you					
6. Spent 15 minutes enjoying the outdoors					
7. Ate a healthy meal					
8. Engaged in intentional breathing or prayer					
9. Let go of something you can't control					
10. Told yourself something kind about yourself					
11. Engaged in a creative activity					
12. Laughed authentically and deeply					
Total points per day					

Conclusion

"God has a funny way of showing you lessons."
— *Eric Roberson*

While I did not initially set out to write a book about resilience, I always knew I wanted to share what I have learned through my challenges (and mistakes). At the new-student orientation session of my doctoral program in 2007, I was asked to envision my dream for ten years post-graduation. I said, "I want to author a book so good that Oprah will list it on her list of favorite reads."

Well, I don't know if Oprah will ever read this, but I still hold onto the aspiration that this work will be valuable to people who need it most.

I have been working on this book for many years and have carried some guilt about taking so long. But taking my time has offered the opportunity to weave a tapestry of reflection, analysis, evidence-based research, and student testimonials. The result is a literary exploration that is part memoir, part textbook, and part activity guide. I hope that by sharing my stories of failure and forgiveness, growth and gratitude, I will help someone find encouragement through a relatable experience.

The fifteen lessons shared here are not exhaustive. There is much more I can and will someday share. For today, for right now, I am declaring this enough. I must remind myself each day that I do enough, I give enough, I care enough, and I am enough.

Dedication

This book is dedicated to my late husband, Scott A. Robinson. He was a champion for my work and my life. Scott physically left this Earth too soon, but his spirit remains strongly present in our lives and our hearts. For forty-seven years, he demonstrated extraordinary resilience. In the face of painful sickle cell disease episodes, Scott taught us how to create joy in a life filled with uncertainty and adversity. Many of the lessons I learned from him are reflected in this book. It has been more than twelve years since he passed away, but I hear his voice in my head at nearly every turn.

This book would not have been possible without the support and insight of my mother, Bonita. She bestowed upon me her writing talent. More importantly, she modeled resilience throughout her life. Born into a family of violence, alcoholism, and all forms of abuse, she has shown the world that it is possible to break intergenerational cycles of dysfunction. When I look at her now, it is difficult to imagine the adversity she experienced throughout her life. She is so strong, capable, confident, and clear about her values. I aspire to be as extraordinary as she is.

I am so grateful to my adopted father, Wayne. He taught me that kinfolk goes beyond bloodlines and has everything to do with love. Through his unrelenting care and concern, despite his parents' disdain for me, I learned to believe in myself. Since his passing in 2015, I have missed the cards of encouragement he sent to keep me in active pursuit of my goals. The memories of his spirit keep me going, as I can still hear him beamingly say, "Wow, I am so proud of you."

I am grateful for all I have learned as a parent, godparent, and grandparent. As a single parent twice, I have learned that while I need to keep working on myself, I am okay with all my imperfections because I am doing the best I can. Through my children and grandchildren, I am learning to be a better listener, to be less judgmental, and to be more discerning. I am learning to let go and let God, and to resist doing for others what they should do for themselves.

I am also indebted to my current husband, Wesley, who is a relentless and patient cheerleader, friend, advisor, and supporter of my success. He has taught me a great deal about life, myself, and the world around us. In our seven years together, I have learned to love myself even more deeply because of the unconditional love he shows me every day.

I also want to express my deepest appreciation for the wonderful circle of friends who have graced my life over the years. They, too, are my kinfolk who had my back through rough times and joined me in countless celebrations. They taught me so much about prioritization, commitment, and self-respect.

I am also extremely thankful to the 210 students who participated in my Strategies for Building Resilience course from 2020 to 2025 and all the guest speakers who made it an amazing experience. They have taught me so much about putting resilience skills and strategies into practice and given me so much inspiration to walk my talk.

Most of all, I give thanks to my Creator for the gifts of cognition, articulation, empathy, and determination. Through my faith walk, I have learned to forgive, love, and embrace the stories of others who help me be a better person.

References

Allport, G. (1954). *The Nature of Prejudice.* Cambridge: Perseus.

Anderson, H. (1965). *The ugly duckling.* New York: Charles Scribner's Sons.

Bandura, A. (1997). *Self-efficacy: The exercise of control.* New York: W. H. Freeman and Company.

Benight, C., & Bandura, A. (2004). Social cognitive theory of post-traumatic recovery: The role of perceived self-efficacy. *Behaviour Research and Therapy, 42*(10), 1129–1148.

Benight, C., Shoji, K., James, L., Waldrep, E., D. D., & Cieslak, R. (2015). Trauma Coping Self-Efficacy: A context-specific self-efficacy measure for traumatic stress. *Psychological Trauma: Theory, Research, Practice, and Policy, 7*(6), 591-599.

Brach, T. (2004). *Radical Acceptance: Embracing Your Life With the Heart of a Buddha.* New York City: Random House.

Bridges, W., & Bridges, S. (2019). *Transitions: Making Sense of Life's Changes.* (40th Anniversary ed.). Da Capo Lifelong Books.

Brown, B. (2012). *Dare to Lead.* New York: Penguin Random House.

Bryant, F., & Veroff, J. (2017). *Savoring: A New Model of Positive Experience.* New York: Psychology Press.

Cabrera, B. (2015). *Beyond Happy: Women, Work, and Well-being.* Association for Talent Development.

Calhoun, L., & Tedeschi, R. (2006). *Handbook of posttraumatic growth: Research and practice.* Lawrence Erlbaum Associates Publishers.

Cooperrider, D., & Whitney, D. (2005). *Appreciative Inquiry: A Positive Revolution in Change.* New York: Berrett-Koehler.

Dweck, C. (2016). *Mindset: the new psychology of success.* New York: Random House.

Evidence Based EFT. (2024). *What is EFT "Tapping"?* Retrieved from Evidence Based EFT: https://www.evidencebasedeft. com/what-is-eft-tapping

Frankl, V. (2006). *Man's Search for Meaning.* Boston: Beacon Press.

Hersey, T. (2022). *Rest Is Resistance: A Manifesto.* Little, Brown Spark.

hooks, b. (2003). *Rock my soul: Black people and self-esteem.* New York: Atria.

Hoopes, L. (2017). *Prosilience: Building Your Resilience for a Turbulent World.* Dara Press.

International, S. G. (2025, August 3). *The Meaning of Nam-myo-ho-renge-kyo*. Retrieved from Practicing Buddhism: https://www.sokaglobal.org/resources/study-materials/buddhist-concepts/the-meaning-of-nam-myoho-renge-kyo.html

Ito, M. (n.d.). Retrieved from https://www.mitsukoito.com/

Kirimura, Y. (1993). *The Fundamentals of Buddhism.* Nichiren Shoshu International Center.

Maté, G. (2019). *When the Body Says No The Cost of Hidden Stress.* Toronto, CA: Vintage Canada.

McArthur-Blair, J., & Cockell, J. (2018). *Building Resilience with Appreciative Inquiry.* Oakland: Berrett-Koehler.

Mental Health America. (2024). *Co-Dependency*. Retrieved from Mental Health America: mhnational.org

Neff, K. (2023). Self-Compassion: Theory, Method, Research, and Intervention. *Annual Review of Psychology, 74*, pp. 193–218. doi:https://doi.org/10.1146/annurev-psych-032420-031047

Nhất Hạnh, T. (1997). *Living Buddha Living Christ.* Chicago: Penguin.

Ong, A., Edwards, L., & Bergeman, C. (2006). Hope as a source of resilience in later adulthood. *Personality and Individual Differences*, 1263–1273.

Rotter, J. B. (1954). *Social learning and clinical psychology.* New York: Prentice Hall.

Seligman, M. E. (1967). Failure to escape traumatic shock. *Journal of Experimental Psychology, 74*(1), 74(1), 1–9.

Tao, T., Yung, Y., Tung Lau, A., Liu, H., Liang, L., Bryant, F., & Hou, W. (Feb 2024). Savoring mediates the mental health benefits of positive coping processes: A prospective population-based analysis. *Applied Psychology: Health and Well-Being*, 1-394.

The Bible: King James Version. (n.d.).

Tolle, E. (2004). *The power of now: A guide to spiritual enlightenment.* Vancouver: Namaste Publishing.

Van der Kolk, B. (2014). *The Body Keeps the Score: Brain, Mind, and Body in the Healing of Trauma.* New York: Viking.

Walsch, N. (1995). *Conversations with God an uncommon dialogue.* New York: G.P. Putman's Sons.

Willock, K. (2024). *How to say no to an addict.* Retrieved from Treehouse Recovery Services: YouTube

The Resilience FIRST Model™

Find your locus of control

Lesson #1: Let go of what you can't control
Lesson #2: Find points of influence
Lesson #3: Take ownership of what you can control

Investigate and manage fear

Lesson #4: Identify the source of your fear
Lesson #5: Calm the fear-center of your brain
Lesson #6: Generate hopeful and optimistic thoughts

Reprogram Unhealthy Conditioning

Lesson #7: Pay attention to your inner voice
Lesson #8: Focus on your strengths
Lesson #9: Savor the good

Seek healthy support

Lesson #10: Talk to those who have "seen the movie"
Lesson #11: Define your circles of trust
Lesson #12: Nurture your spirituality

Take time for self-care

Lesson #13: Set healthy boundaries
Lesson #14: Prioritize rest
Lesson #15: Stack healthy habits